G

'Harding is a self-deprecating and winsome writer whose bittersweet musings on middle-age, loneliness and the search for spiritual enlightenment ... are leavened by an incredibly dry and unforced wit' *Metro Herald*

'Often funny, occasionally disturbing and not without its moments of deep sadness, Harding has peeled back his soul and held it out on the palm of his hand for all to see' Christine Dwyer-Hickey

'A repository of modern man's deepest fears, Harding emerges as something of an embattled hero for our times ... It's rare for a memoir to demand such intense emotional involvement, and rarer still for it to be so fully rewarded' *The Sunday Times*

'Hilarious, and tender, and mad, and harrowing, and wistful, and always beautifully written. A wonderful book' Kevin Barry

'I read this book in one sitting ... Beautifully written ... *Staring at Lakes* gives us permission to be lost, sick, sad, creative, happy and compassionate – in short, to be human' Mary McEvoy, *Irish Independent*

'This memoir grabs you from the outset and holds you right to the end. His language sings' Deirdre Purcell

'Written in lyrical prose, it provides a compelling insight into the turbulent emotions that rage behind so many of the bland faces we meet in everyday life' *Sunday Business Post*

Michael Harding is an author and playwright. His creative chronicle of ordinary life in the Irish midlands is published as a weekly column in *The Irish Times*. He has written numerous plays for the Abbey Theatre, including *Una Pooka*, *Misogynist* and *Sour Grapes*, and has published three novels, *Priest*, *The Trouble with Sarah Gullion* and *Bird in the Snow* as well as two bestselling memoirs, *Staring at Lakes* and *Hanging with the Elephant*.

Talking to Strangers

And other ways of being human

MICHAEL HARDING

HACHETTE
BOOKS
IRELAND

First published in Ireland in 2016 by
HACHETTE BOOKS IRELAND

I

Cataloguing in Publication Data is available from the British Library.

The Field © 1966 John B Keane.
Reprinted by kind permission of Mercier Press Ltd., Cork.

Some of the reflections have previously appeared in
Michael Harding's Irish Times column.

ISBN: 9781473623576

Typeset in Adobe Garamond by Bookends Publishing Services
Printed and bound in Great Britain by Clays Ltd, St Ives plc

Hachette Books Ireland policy is to use papers that are natural, renewable
and recyclable products and made from wood grown in sustainable forests.
The logging and manufacturing processes are expected to conform to the
environmental regulations of the country of origin.

Hachette Books Ireland
8 Castlecourt Centre, Castleknock, Dublin 15, Ireland

A division of Hachette UK Ltd
Carmelite House, 50 Victoria Embankment, London, EC4Y 0DZ

www.hachettebooksireland.ie

For Simon

Some of the names and details in this book have been changed to protect the privacy of individuals.

Contents

The Ending:
The Mystery of Love

I love washing machines. It's not that I use them a lot but the spinning world of linen, cotton and wool always assures me that there's someone else in the house. I am not alone. Especially when it spins and begins to whine like a sean-nós singer reaching a high note.

When the beloved was away, I didn't use it very often. I abandoned dirty clothes wherever they fell, which led to problems when I ran out of underwear. But briefs, vests and socks are so cheap that it was easier to buy new ones than waste money on washing powder, the only problem being that the mountain of laundry got bigger and bigger.

So the solution was not to use the machine except when necessary and, for months, I rarely washed anything.

The only time it is worth washing clothes is when her stuff is in the basket. That has erotic possibilities. Women's clothes are overpowering. I remember times in my student days when a naked bra hanging out of a laundry basket in a girlfriend's bathroom would drive me wild with desire. But at my age, I prefer to avoid that sort of emotional intensity for health reasons.

One day after she came home, I went into the house and said to her 'I'm thinking of putting on a wash. Do you have anything for the basket?'

She had just arrived from Warsaw.

In fact, she had a whole lot of things.

'They're all in my bag,' she said. 'It's in the kitchen.'

The sky was blue and I decided to spend the day working through the lot. The machine was never off and, by evening time, there was a great pile of white things on the kitchen table, which I moved lovingly to the line outside.

But I only did that once. I did it because it was such an overwhelming joy to see her home after being away for so long. To do it every week or every second day would be another matter. I did it because I had been broken-hearted by her absence. And when she came home, I was ecstatic. And the ritual of lifting her items one by one onto the clothesline drove me into a delirium of joy.

I knew a man one time who was broken-hearted by the loss of his wife. He was sixty-one and after she moved out he took up the piano.

I asked him was he any good.

He said, 'No.'

We were sitting in his drawing room at the time, the same one he had shared with her for thirty years. He played the scales for me.

4

Then he said, 'You know, I should practise more.'

I said, 'You're sixty-one; it's time to stop practising.'

'She went a year ago,' he said, 'but the good weather last week reminded me of the time we cycled around Ireland in 1994.'

He'd first met her when he was cycling on the Lynn Road near Mullingar in 1958. Her bicycle had had a flat tyre. That autumn he invited her to a concert.

'It was the Hallé Orchestra,' he said. 'They were playing Elgar – in Mullingar. Imagine that!'

A few years ago, they went to the National Concert Hall 5 for the first time and, about a week later, they were outside SuperValu when she told him.

'It was so sudden,' he said, 'like an amputation! I didn't even know how to use the washing machine when she was gone.'

My beloved was only gone away to study, and she came back after nine months, but when she saw all her clothes on the line, interspersed with my vests and socks, she knew something was wrong. The line billowed in a warm June breeze. She stood looking at it and then at me.

'What have you done?' she enquired.

'I did the washing,' I said.

'But you never do the washing,' she said.

'I know,' I agreed. 'But you're home. I couldn't help myself.'

6   Solitude is a place I go to sometimes – it's like a room inside me. In there, I lose all curiosity for anything except my own existence.

It's called existential anxiety. It's called philosophy. Sometimes it's just a way of avoiding other people; but entanglement with others *is* the most essential condition for happiness. I do it regularly. I drift away. I forget who is in the room with me. And it feels like it will never end. I hug the little fire in the stove. I hug something inside myself and don't look outwards.

And then spring comes. The beloved comes. The entanglement with others grows under my feet again like fresh grass and I start all over, to love, and cut flowers, and sing in her presence. Others are not so lucky.

I remember walking on the beach at Banna Strand many years ago with another friend whose marriage had broken down.

Everything comes to an end, he joked, but the way he said it was disillusioned and bitter. He felt alone. The beach stretched for miles and we were like twigs under the vast canopy of grey cloud. We walked like old men, hauling ourselves into the wind. The empty space suited us as we staggered over the dunes.

I raked the sand with my fingers at one stage and let it run through them and fall into the wind and be carried away.

I remember him before he grew old and bald. He had a Nepalese cardigan bought in an Oxfam shop in London, and he wore a rainbow-coloured hat on his curly hair and he had a beard. But, over the years, he grew aloof with his insulated wounds.

Eventually, his wife despaired. She ran off with the postman, leaving a declaration of resentment on the kitchen table and a solicitor's letter which was the opening volley in a decade of litigation.

It's not quite what they had promised each other when they were teenagers, paddling in the lake, swinging their legs on the wall beside the bus station.

As he drove away after our walk on the beach, he said, 'I don't know how your wife puts up with you.'

When he was gone, I thought, Neither do I. But I suppose that's the mystery.

The Beginning:
A Paradise of Small Things

Maybe it all began to fall apart for me around the time of my neighbour's death. It was at the end of 2014. He was a good neighbour, and when he died, a part of me died too.

That's why I started worrying again. Tunnelling into anxiety. Looking at my beloved as if I wasn't certain of her love. Walking around the garden, worrying if the trees might all die some day, and looking at our little cottage and wondering when it might crumble or if the roof was about to fall in.

I had been living in a solid world. My beloved had been my anchor for years. And our home was a paradise of small things that we could rely on. The open fire. The bottle of wine. The snow at Christmas. The eyes of a child. The company of friends. The regularity of the farmer next door completing his chores season after season.

We lived in an unchanging world and we watched him through the seasons moving cattle or mowing meadows or lodging bales of silage into the rusting red shed to the south of our land. We sat on the porch, holding hands, sipping wine and listening to the sound of the tractor in the distance. I thought about how we would not even have been there if it had not been for him.

My memories of those early years are all sweet and vivid. When we came to the hill for the first time a wonderful world opened up for us. It was a time of mowing grass, of cutting hay, of swallows flying low across the face of the lawn. Of fledgling birds falling out of nests. Of liquid blackbirds leading the dawn chorus at 5 a.m. Of warm afternoons behind curtains, when the birds outside slept so intensely in the trees that I could imagine them snoring little birdie snores. Of the corncrake in the long grass, in the neighbour's land that bordered ours.

After our neighbour died, I would sit on the patio for hours listening for the tractor that never came. Gazing at the rushes growing in the empty fields.

A shadow drifted across the garden and would not go away. Which was strange as we did not know him very well. We had rarely spoken. But we could never forget the kindness he had done to us. The blessing that he had, by accident, bestowed on our lives.

We were renting an old house outside the village of Keadue. The chimney was cracked and the smoke from the downstairs fire seeped through the walls of the upstairs rooms. We were just married and there was an infant in the cot but, being artists, we had no money and when we went to the building societies and banks in Carrick-on-Shannon the men in suits behind their desks smiled at us politely and asked if we had jobs. We confessed that we were artists and had no steady income at all. And then we were shown the door.

I was convinced that there were only two ways to get money out of a bank. One was to walk in wearing a balaclava and carrying a gun and shoot from the hip, which was something people had done regularly along the border when I was young. The other was to go in wearing a suit and talk from the hip. So I opted for the latter. I would weave a spell around the bank manager about how wonderful I was and how much money I was going to make in the coming years.

I would admit that I was a writer, but would say that film was going to be my future. I would produce figures out of the air, projecting income over five or ten years. I was going to make hundreds of thousands of pounds, I would say.

And then, after a passionate performance, I might ask for a small loan. Maybe £20,000. And since the country was in recession at the time, and Leitrim survived on a black economy and small cottages were being sold off very cheap, that might just be enough to buy a house.

So, in 1994, I sought an appointment with the manager

13

of a bank in Leitrim. And on the day before the meeting I got a call from a junior staff member.

'What is the meeting about?'

'I need money,' I explained.

And she thanked me and said she would call me back to confirm the meeting. But of course when she returned my call, an hour later, it was to cancel. I suppose they thought the manager was too busy to have meetings with an upstart like me: a failed writer who was simply begging for money.

14 'The manager is busy on Tuesday,' she said politely, 'but it's really the loans manager you should be talking to.'

'Oh, that's fine,' I said, 'sure that would be grand.'

I put down the phone, though I was not at all happy with the situation. I didn't sleep well that Monday night and lay in bed from daybreak on Tuesday, trying to imagine what a loans manager might look like. Perhaps it was just a fancy title for some junior official who had the difficult task of assessing people's credit when, like me, they came in cap in hand. If I went to a loans manager, I would be processed and dismissed. Because there was no reason anyone should give me money.

So I phoned the bank again.

'I need to see the manager this morning,' I explained, 'and nobody else.'

'Well, you have an appointment with the loans manager. That's the person you need to be talking to,' she said.

'No,' I said, 'it isn't. And I don't.'

'Don't what?'

'I don't have an appointment with the loans manager. I have an appointment with the manager. That's what I arranged originally.'

There was a pause.

'I want to see the bossman,' I said. 'It's the only option. Is he available or not?'

I was using my best accent, an affected posh tone, hoping that I sounded like the bank manager might need me more than I needed him.

'Please hold,' she said. And to my delight, after being left waiting for a few minutes, she returned to the phone and said that the manager was willing to meet me. I thanked her as if his agreement was the most normal thing in the world. When I got off the phone, I yelped with delight. I put on a green suit, the one I had been married in, and with a briefcase in my hand headed out to battle.

I sat in his office and tried to bamboozle him with talk about the film industry, literary agents and advances for screenplays that I was expecting soon, though I had as yet written no screenplays whatsoever.

He was a stout man with spectacles and a soft, round face. He smiled so warmly from behind his desk that I presumed he knew I was talking rubbish. And when I finished my pitch, we eyeballed each other like gunslingers, each of us waiting for the other to make a move.

He moved first.

'How much do you want?' he asked.

Maybe he was trying to confuse me. I mean, why would he ask such an obvious question?

'20K,' I replied like I was Paul Newman, and I didn't flinch.

He took up a phone and spoke to someone in the next office.

'Joe,' he said, 'could you bring me in forms for a loan account, please? Thanks.'

He smiled at me.

'Jesus, that was quick,' I blurted out, my affected BBC voice gone completely.

He smiled again.

'I do a bit of writing myself,' he explained.

That was all. And so it was done in an instant and I had my money, and perhaps all because I knocked on the door of the only bank manager in Ireland with an imagination and a respect for literature and the guts to give a poor writer a financial start.

I went home to the beloved and we made love against the kitchen table that stood on a floor of bare cement while the child slept in her cot in the only habitable bedroom upstairs.

But we had the money.

When we were young, that's all we longed for. Money. Because we already had all the love we needed. And of

16

course we longed for a house. Which we found one day when the beloved noticed a small cottage for sale in the local newspaper. It stood on five acres of land that sloped eastward towards Lough Allen.

The owner was a farmer who had inherited the cottage and land from a relation who had recently died, and his interest was in the land but not the little cottage, since he lived in a fine two-storey house with his mother just a mile down the road. It was a white pebble-dashed cottage with tiny rooms and small windows and an ugly cement water tank in the back for harvesting rainwater from the roof. That was the only supply to fill the taps or the bath or the cistern for the toilet. But it had a view of the lake, and that was all we wanted. We bought it and began to paint the walls white and construct a wooden shed for fuel outside, and we bought rugs for the living-room floor and linoleum for the kitchen. We lit the white Stanley range that had not been warm since the previous occupant had died and we looked out at the swamp of wild rushes around the house as if we were in paradise.

We planted hardwood trees around the house the following winter, and as the trees began to grow and fill out with leaf, first to knee height and then beyond the reach of my raised arms, we felt a deep gratitude to the man who had sold us the property. There wasn't a day that we didn't see him in the fields around us, tending black cattle or mowing grass or just standing on a headland as still as a bird.

The years passed and the child grew into a young woman and the trees grew tall and green, but the neighbour maintained his pattern as regular as a clock. He was always there.

And after he died, I could still sense his presence in the shadows around the galvanised shed or in the meadow beyond our trees. The hay barn to the south of our land stood silent, but for the wind in the rusty sheets, and Roxie our cat would still go down there and sit in the hay that he had saved the previous year. When I went near the shed, Roxie would come out and rub her back against my leg, pleading with me for attention, as if she were asking something.

Where is he?

He had been a stranger on a tractor when we met him first, a young man who was shy and talked little. On the day we came to look at the house, he was driving his cattle along the mountain road.

He had the keys and he showed us inside, and then he withdrew to the gate and smoked a cigarette, waiting until we were finished.

When we said we loved the house and asked the price, he looked for no enormous profit. When we went back to him two years later and asked would he sell us another small parcel of land, a third of an acre on which to plant more trees, he named another modest price and the solicitors did the rest without fuss. That was twenty years ago. But now he was gone forever.

His fields lay silent all through the winter of 2014, and no sound was heard from his Volkswagen Jetta in the distance. January 2015 came and went in a frozen fog and February was a deluge of rain. I looked out the windows but nothing came up the hill. I never spoke his name, but his absence had become a thing in itself, an emptiness I could almost touch.

19

The beloved would look at me and ask, 'Are you OK?'

And I would say, 'I'm fine. Maybe I just need to go out for a while.'

And then I would get in the car and drive around Leitrim or towards Cavan to pass an hour or two or to cheer myself up by calling on someone I knew.

One morning, I called on a couple I had known for years and who had long ago escaped their middle-class youth to live a new-age life near the lake.

There was no sign of himself when I arrived, and she was standing in the kitchen in a purple dress that smelled of lavender, tea tree oil, basil and marijuana.

As she stirred the basil soup, her partner emerged from

the bedroom, a man with long grey hair, wearing a leather biker's suit, with a helmet and balaclava under his oxter. He looked like he was going out to assassinate someone.

'I'm going for a ride,' he said, cool and understated.

When he was gone, I talked to herself, the long cheesecloth lavender woman, about soups and lentils and how to keep healthy. He returned about an hour later. I heard the muffled sound of the exhaust in the distance, and then, through the kitchen window, I could see him floating back over the hill and up the gravel avenue like a samurai warrior emerging from a movie screen, and my heart sank because I had enjoyed being alone with her, watching her move about the kitchen in her long dress.

He said he had been to Drumshanbo and back. There was something masculine about him in a mythic sort of way that I envied as I nattered with his wife about massage, yoga and meditation, the usual topics that arise with romantics in Leitrim who have unspoken pasts.

But then I mentioned Periscope.

I explained that it was a phone app that enabled people to broadcast live, and that I was fascinated by it.

She said she didn't have a phone and she didn't seem to have any notion what an app was.

The warrior sat in the corner and rolled a joint. He said that phones fry your brains and cause cancer.

He himself was looking very well after his ride: long grey hair to his shoulders and three rings on various fingers.

He wore a faded blue denim shirt underneath his biker's gear, which he had unfurled to his waist, and he had a saffron scarf around his neck.

Given that I didn't seem to realise the evils of mobile phones, he may have felt I needed further education.

'Don't you know,' he enquired, 'that windmills cause draughts? You ever notice that they don't just move in the wind? They actually create the fucking wind!'

I said I didn't think that was possible.

'Oh, indeed it is,' he said.

'But,' I said, 'the windmills generate electricity from the wind. They're not generating the wind. That wouldn't be economical.'

'The fact is that they move, even on days when there is no wind,' he explained, with enormous eyes staring at me. 'Ask yourself. Why is the government subsidising them?'

'That's amazing,' I said, 'if it's true.'

'But there's more,' he added.

'More?'

'Yes. I was talking to a documentary maker the other night in Manorhamilton, and he's doing a film about it. Apparently there's a possibility that the government intends storing gas in them which will be released at night and the windmills will act as fans to spread the gas across vast layers of mountain bog.'

'Why?' I wondered.

'Pesticides,' he replied. 'It's all about preserving the bogs, like what the EU does with the lettuce. That's why the turf cutting has been banned. They're going to use windmills to spread chemical weed killer so they have to get people off the bogs. If you're living close to the windmills you won't know what's coming out of them at night.'

There was a pause. He sucked on the joint. It was only noon and he was already as confused as my cat.

'Are you living close to any windmills?' he wondered.

I didn't answer. I tried to focus on the soup and the woman in the long dress. She had beautiful nut-brown hair and the rich, pungent odour from her clothes was intoxicating me, and the soup she placed in front of me was full of little bits of everything, and it tasted spicy and delicious.

After a morning like that, I'd often spend the afternoon on the couch watching recorded episodes of *Judge Judy*. I didn't walk much in the garden. It's something I used to do before I grew melancholic, but not any longer.

The fields held their own melancholy now, and soon the rushes would grow on the fields he had mown, and the mountain wilderness of hogweed and gorse would creep back in through the gates and return the land to its unruly origins, as if no man had ever lived or toiled there for all those years.

The summer sky was always full of sound in Leitrim, from the booming bittern to the cry of the curlew, but

22

there was no sound as delicious as our neighbour's tractor in a field nearby, as he sat steering and twisting his head to watch the rake toss the mown grass into perfect lines behind him, and later the thump of hay bales being piled into the red galvanised shed, where the cat moved in his wake as she hunted for field mice.

In November fog, he would drive up the hills with bales of hay sticking out of the boot of his Volkswagen to feed the cattle that were waiting for him in the fields.

And later he would move them to lower ground, driving the Volkswagen behind them slowly, his hand out the window, gently banging the outside of the car door to nudge the animals farther down the lane, animals that were as calm and quiet as himself. And like many rural men, he wasn't given to overexcitement. He'd raise one finger from the steering wheel to salute me. If I whispered my enthusiasm for the good weather as we passed, he might agree, but he would cautiously add, 'Will it last?'

I remember watching him one summer evening when he had finished his work and the sloping grass had been shaved to its yellow roots; he stood alone on the brow of the hill. He was having one last look at the field. And the smoke of his cigarette dissolved in the air around his head. I said to myself, there's a man who is satisfied with his work. There's a man who is proud of his land.

The little church in Arigna was so full for his funeral that I couldn't get in, so I stood with dozens of other men outside, on a dry day in November. The slanting sun cut into our faces as the coffin was shouldered towards the cemetery.

It was no big deal. People were just there to witness the closure of a simple life. To celebrate a quiet man who walked deeply on the earth and loved its colours.

When a farmer dies in the countryside, there is a strange emptiness in the fields. They grow ragged with rushes, and, without paint, the galvanised sheds turn to rust after a few years, then, eventually, the forestry arrives and all trace of human habitation is swallowed by the dark woods.

Those of us who live in the hills above Lough Allen had lost another solitary man. And all across the west of Ireland it was the same; one by one the lights were going out.

Our neighbour's death changed something in me.

It would not be possible to go on as before, as if we were young, having barbecues and waving at the world like young people do. Our neighbour was the closest human being to us in the isolated world of rural Ireland where we had found our paradise. Though he never spoke much with us, we could feel and see his love in the fields and in the cattle, every day of the year.

I didn't tell the beloved I was brooding. All through the winter of 2014, and the spring and summer of 2015, I pushed myself hard. I kept myself busy. I travelled to Romania and toured Ireland and worked on a play in Dublin just to feel alive. To feel connected.

But each time it was the opposite.

I felt more and more distant from others. Even my beloved became a stranger while we were still sitting on the couch together. Until eventually in the summer of 2015, sitting at the breakfast table with boiled eggs and her trying to get the shell off her egg without burning her fingers, she suddenly said it.

'I need to go away. But it will only be for nine months.'

I said, 'Oh, yeah, sure that's fine.'

25

Inside, I was thinking, That's not fine. Everything is going to fall apart now. Just like the philosophers say. I didn't know if I could manage on my own.

I feared that nine months might be long enough for a couple to drift apart. And that this might be the beginning of a separation. And that the permanence of our paradiso in the little cottage might be disintegrating.

But if it was, what could I do?

The universe unfolds and events arise, and things change and the cookie always crumbles in the end. That's life.

26   The beloved had been coming and going to Poland for about three years. Although it wasn't her that started it. It was me who first took a fancy to snow. It was me who had a Polish ancestor and who couldn't resist cheap flights to Warsaw, and it was me who pleaded with her to come one winter for a week to Warsaw. She agreed and we spent our time in a sauna in the Sofihotel and on the streets of snow and in the art galleries. We wandered through parks of trees, and visited churches and museums, and ate traditional Polish food in various restaurants.

And I think it was the light in the winter sky that drew me there. The crisp earth, the white rooftops, the snow covering the parks and the regularity of blue heavens that drew me away from the bleak Irish winter and the rain-drenched afternoons when Leitrim lingered in a state of semi-permanent twilight.

But it was she who broke the ice socially one evening in

an art gallery where a contemporary artist was exhibiting new work. She clinked her glass of wine with a stranger and, before I knew it, she was in the middle of a circle of crusty-looking Polish painters. As fellow artists, they got on splendidly even without sharing a common language. Before the week was up, she had immersed herself in a network of artists living and working in the city.

That was in 2012. Each year, she has gone to Warsaw for a little longer. She has had exhibitions there. She has found it possible to work creatively in the solitude of snow, surrounded by a foreign language.

27

But it was only when she announced at the breakfast table that she was going for nine months that I really took notice.

Later that day, we were looking across the lake towards the mountain on the far side, at the little houses in the crevice of the mountain that cluster along the Dowra road and around the village of Ballinaglera, when she mentioned it again. 'Do you remember what I was talking about at breakfast?'

But I wasn't paying her attention because I saw a light. It came through the clouds and it lit up the village and the green fields and ditches and the roadway on the far side of the water. The rest of the lakeshore was in shadow but this singular light on the far shoreline absorbed me.

Ballinaglera means 'the town of the clerics'. There had been a monastic site there as early as the sixth century. And

I was trying to imagine someone fifteen hundred years ago standing where I was standing and seeing exactly what I was seeing.

That's what I was doing as she spoke. I was drifting into solitude. I was dropping away from her voice, my ears hearing only the deliciously abstract sounds she made. I was sweeping a space clean inside myself. A place where I was alone even if I was in the middle of a conversation with her. She was saying that she was thinking of going to Warsaw for almost a year.

28   She may have said it twice. She may have said that as an artist she had work to do and that she needed to be in Warsaw for nine months. Maybe longer. And maybe she said more, but I wasn't listening. I was watching the light on the water, and thinking how wonderful it was to be with her, and how all would be well forever between us if only we could just stay in our little cottage in the hills above Lough Allen.

In the autumn of 2015, she left from Carrick-on-Shannon train station and, afterwards, I sat in the kitchen imagining her journey – drinking a coffee in the rickety, rattling carriage or eating a Danish pastry perhaps. Imagining her seated in the plane at take off as the steward demonstrated how to wear a seat belt.

And I was left in a house upturned by builders. With

half-painted walls. With dirty floors and sawdust heaped in the corners. Wires were sticking out of the walls, though the electrician had promised he would be finished the following week. It was always next week. And, at night, I consoled myself with *The Good Wife* and *Judge Judy* on the television.

I filled a bucket with ashes from the stove each morning. And a heap of chopped wood stood inside the door. The gales of rain lashed a single pair of socks that hung on the line. The bed linen had not been changed for weeks. I followed other people's lives as they appeared on Facebook. I read posts about the wonderful times everyone else was enjoying, such happy parties and anniversaries they were preparing, and how everyone was so overwhelmed by all their friends.

I stared at blank pages on my computer screen and sensed that I ought to be writing something but I couldn't get started. And then I stared at the picture on the wall.

It was a photograph of my great-grandmother, staring back at me and monitoring my gradual decline through self-pity and rage into a kind of a numb loneliness, a lethargy that inhibited me from wiping yesterday's crumbs or stale shards of cheese from the kitchen table.

While the beloved was where?

Gone! Up and away on Ryanair like a youthful backpacker, like a young thing recently released from the mortifications of school.

What she would do after the plane landed I couldn't imagine. Maybe she wasn't going to work on her art at all. Maybe she'd crash out with some young male model and go to discos and raves and drink all night for weeks in late-night vodka parlours and live in free abandonment, as artists sometimes do. Fine. Maybe years of living in Leitrim had damaged her mind the way it had damaged me before I fled to Mullingar. I too had imagined an escape to the sophistication of Europe. Although I didn't get very far. She, on the other hand, had succeeded in connecting with artists, real artists out there in the exotic icy streets of a city that Hitler had once bombed into the Stone Age and which the citizens had rebuilt with faith and courage and the help of old medieval paintings. It was certainly more exciting than my little adventures in Mullingar.

And when she had walked out the door she had left my universe; she was singing her own songs in some unknown elsewhere, and I had to make do with the ashes and the whispering stove, the bronchial cat and the distant hammer on scaffolding breaking through the fog.

I shared my feelings about all this with the General on one occasion.

'That's not unusual,' he said. 'The fact is she has abandoned you! So just find someone else. Immediately! It's as simple as that.'

'You're mad,' I replied.

'Only as an interim solution, of course,' he added. 'It will solve your isolation problem. That's all. Don't waste time watching television. Get out there and meet women. Get laid! There is someone in the world waiting for you.'

I put down the phone before he lost the run of himself, and I stood looking around the room, trying to calm myself. But everything in the room, and everything in the house, was connected to the beloved in one way or another. There wasn't a dish or tray or cushion that was not connected to her. We had shared a space for too long. We had woven our narrative into the very fabric of the house.

And it's ironic how the objects and spaces a couple share can become a trap when one half is left behind. I've often seen it in the faces of bereaved friends. Men standing in kitchens of crockery that they cannot bear to touch after a funeral. Women sniffing suits in the wardrobe of a room where they once made love. The absence of a partner shimmering in the shapelessness of an old pair of trousers hanging on a chair or a shirt forgotten in the laundry basket.

The dead come to us, garishly in the emptiness, in their discarded clothes and toiletries, creating an airless absence from which there is no escape. No wonder some cultures burn the house, the home or the caravan after a death to cleanse the world of all memory, all remnant of the partner's story, and ease the pain of those who are left behind.

It occurred to me when she was gone that all our useless

31

things could one day turn on us too. The nick-nacks that we had exchanged on Christmas mornings or at times of birth or significant anniversaries might someday lie there, wasted in the dust, when one of us is left to stagger on alone.

The thoughts were terrifying. So I drank. And watched TV. And drank more. And lay in bed till noon each day.

On the other hand, she would be out there in Warsaw somewhere, free from all this shared narrative. She was single in her new world, unhindered by domestic paraphernalia or the collection of useless things that a man obsesses over and then discards in every nook and cranny of the house.

Perhaps I flashed into her mind too as she walked along Nowy Świat Street or sat in a restaurant in Warsaw's Old Town eating pierogi. Who is to say?

32

The Deaths of Strangers

The death of a stranger can unsettle us, sometimes as much as the loss of a loved one. I remember something similar happening to Natalia, the Russian girl who worked in a restaurant in Mullingar and fell in love with my mother.

We used to talk about grannies. It started when my mother was still mobile and I would bring her from the nursing home into town for lunch. Natalia would wait patiently behind the counter for my mother to choose the chicken Kiev or the bacon and cabbage. My mother was slow and Natalia was kind. She cried when my mother died. She said my mother reminded her of her own granny in St Petersburg and I suppose she was homesick. But it created a kind of intimacy between us, so that after my mother died I would still visit the restaurant for a bowl of soup and a slice of homemade brown bread, and I would talk to Natalia because I missed my mother and sitting with her was like having a sister.

'Do you remember your grandmother?' Natalia asked me one day.

'Yes,' I said, 'I do. She was an icon of rural Ireland: a perfect country woman, big and fat, in a black dress and a speckled apron, who put sugar on my bread at the table of her dark kitchen on Bridge Street in Cavan. She died when I was nine.

'I was there when it happened. She was saying that everything was going dark. That she couldn't see anyone. That someone had put the lights out, though it was only the middle of the day. Everyone was fussing around the bed and kneeling down and saying prayers. I stood on the stairs, at a distance from the bedroom door.'

'Ah, yes,' Natalia said, 'I understand.'

I can still remember the dark little kitchen, with its big black range, and her pots and black kettles, with their long spouts like swans' necks and huge black handles. I used to sit in her rocking chair as a boy, before the flickering red coals behind the grille in the range. It was as close as I got in childhood to some kind of heavenly peace.

Natalia understood this too. She used to say that she could still smell the soup from her own grandmother's kitchen on the far side of Europe.

We talked so much about Cavan that one day I decided to take her there for lunch. I insisted that she deserved a day out after all the soups she had made for me in her restaurant in Mullingar. I brought her to Bridge Street and showed her the house where my mother had grown up and then to the Farnham Arms, because that's where I had often gone with mother and where, as a little boy, I had first learned to dance.

'I was twelve years old, all hair oil and sweaty palms, and my fingers barely touched my partner's shoulders as we waddled around the floor.'

Natalia laughed as if she too shared some similar memory.

'In fact my mother also danced in this hotel,' I added.

Natalia was delighted, and then I produced a photograph of my mother from my wallet: a bride, stepping out of a big American car, on her wedding day in 1950; and my own granny standing to attention at the hotel door in a big hat.

'Look,' I said to Natalia. 'That's my grandmother. And that's my mother.'

Natalia seemed sad for a young person. Even when we were sitting together in the hotel looking at the photographs, she seemed to be in the grip of old ghosts, and I realised that we were similar.

In the foyer of the Farnham Arms, we talked long into the afternoon about St Petersburg and her childhood and she told me stories about her grandmother and about snow and love and despair. Stories that made me feel I was in a Russian novel.

'I am very grateful to you,' I said, 'for sharing all this with me.'

'No, don't say that!' she said. 'I have done nothing for you.'

But she had. She had revealed her heart to me. And she had cared for my mother, and the sorrow she had felt at being parted from her own grandmother was obvious in her face. It was as if she had lost part of her soul when she had left Russia, and she carried her exile with great dignity. She didn't tell me why she had been forced to leave her homeland but she did tell me that the sense of loss was like a brick in her stomach that was always present.

38 She told me that her grandfather had fought in the siege of St Petersburg and that it was a beautiful city. And that before he left home the last thing he had said to his beloved was that he would miss her soup.

Natalia opened the door into the world of exiles, emigrants, ancestors and all the other forgottens of history. We talked of mothers, grandmothers, fathers and a variety of other strangers. Of Russians and Poles and Irish folk who wandered from home and died in exile, of people who ended their lives in wars and famines and concentration camps around the globe; all long gone from the earth, except for the space we gave to their memory.

And she made Russia sound romantic. I would say, 'I'd love to go to Poland.' But she would say, 'No, Poland is not nice. Don't go there. You must come to Russia.'

But I said, 'No, I'm not going to Russia. I want to see Poland.'

I didn't realise it at the time but she had roused in me a curiosity for my own ancestors. Not my grandmother in Cavan or her tribe. But a woman called Martha who fled her homeland in Poland many years earlier and came to Dublin. A woman remembered only as the 'German woman', who poked her nose under the lids of her daughter-in-law's pots to ensure her son was being well fed.

'She was Polish,' my father whispered. 'She was Polish.' And he ought to have known since she reared him.

It was a winter's night shortly after our neighbour's death. I was sitting by the fire and my beloved was reading a book and my great-grandmother was staring at me from the wall. It was just a photograph, the only evidence that my father's grandmother had existed. Born in destitution in the slums of Dublin's Liberties, my father was an orphan from infancy and was reared by his granny. He kept her photograph on the wall of the house I grew up in, and I remember him sometimes gazing at her with affection. In the faded black and white image, she seems no older than a teenager. She has curly hair in a bun above her head, and she wears a dark, elegant gown with a tight bodice and puffed up arms, and a chain for a watch falls from below her neck to a tiny pocket at the waist. The picture remained with me many years after my father died, and there it hung on the wall, in 2014, on a night in late November, and as I looked at her she spoke to me.

'Polish,' she whispered, just as my father had whispered. I said nothing.

'But you don't know the half of it,' she added. 'I was wiped out. My story was lost. Not a trace of it remains. Just as nothing will remain of your story in the end. Or your beloved's. Or indeed your neighbour's.'

I was impressed that she knew about the neighbour. And what she said is true. I have spent my life telling stories and yet, like everyone else on the planet, I'll vanish into thin air when I'm dead. The world doesn't really remember the dead. There are too many of them.

Even an attic full of manuscripts that I have sweated over down the years will be lost. The clunky glass and brass trophies and awards I have won for plays, books or performances that gather dust on the shelves won't mean anything in the passing of time.

The idea that a book lifts an author up among the everlasting ones is a fantasy that a writer soon discovers when his books go out of print and he finds them in some second-hand shop selling for a few cents.

The Polish woman on the wall fascinated me. And how her story had been forgotten. And how ironic it was that while the beloved was in Poland, I was at home talking to a photograph and trying to survive as best I could with a washing machine I didn't use.

But even when the beloved was in the house, reading stuff on her iPad by the fire, I'd have one eye on the wall and, sure enough, the Polish woman would still whisper things only I could hear. Because the Polish woman was a myth. She only existed in my psyche, and the more I clung to her, the more sheltered I was in a kind of monastic solitude.

In the old days, monks lived in solitude because they thought it was a way of getting close to God. But I was awake to the existential nature of things. I sensed in my ageing bones the emptiness that the universe holds. So, for me, solitude was no consolation. Solitude was disturbing. And it exhausted me in the absence of the beloved. The wind screeching across the sky and threatening to fell the tall Scots pines outside and rattling the tiles on the rooftop.

Even when the beloved was beside me in the bed, I felt the same. If she woke before me and went to the kitchen to make coffee, I felt abandoned.

And my neighbour's death was just another sign, a moment in the process of change by which the cookie and me and all else was beginning to crumble into dust.

On the first day of December 2014, just a week after our neighbour died, I took a box from the attic and examined its contents. It belonged to my father and, apart from the photograph of Martha, which I had already rescued and put up on the wall, the box was all that remained of his story: birth certs, references, business cards and random cuttings from newspapers. Every few years, I rummaged through it, as if the contents might magically change and I would discover something new.

But always I found the same old things, including a faded receipt for the internment of Martha Frith in the Church of Ireland cemetery of Taney Parish in Dublin, the exact location of the grave written in black ink. But this old information suddenly gave me a new idea.

The next morning, I phoned the parish office whose letterhead was on the burial receipt. A bright, cheerful woman answered, wishing me a happy Christmas.

'I'm looking for the person who keeps records of the graveyard,' I said. 'Is there such a person?'

'Yes, there certainly is,' she said, 'and he just happens to be here beside me. Would you hold the line, please?' And then she put him on.

'How can I help you?' he asked.

'I'm looking for a relative,' I said. 'She was buried years ago but I have all the details.'

'I will have to look it up,' he said. 'I don't have the books to hand.'

44 'And I was also wondering,' I continued, 'if it would be possible to visit the cemetery sometime and have a look at the plot. The number of the grave is on the receipt.'

'Yes, of course,' he said. And we made an appointment for the following week.

It was Monday. I drove up a winding hill near Dundrum to a cemetery surrounded by old stone walls, with a wide footpath near the gates. I parked and shook hands with a tall elderly gentleman who was waiting for me with a ledger under his arm.

He unlocked the old gate and we passed through, taking a soft grass avenue between the ancient stones and yew trees and memorial slabs until we came to a slope where the graves had no headstones at all. Nothing remained of the dead except tiny mounds of earth like a basket of hidden eggs. It was a small and intimate place, undisturbed but for the crows on a yew tree.

I followed the sexton until he stopped at a particular grave close to the yew tree. It was only a green hillock, a dainty green curve on the earth.

'Right,' the sexton said, 'this is it. This is 516.' He intoned the number from the ledger with a certain solemnity. I stared at the grass, trying, in my mind, to link the picture on the wall with the white bones that might lie beneath the soil.

'516,' he repeated. 'That's your grave.'

45

But I could not imagine the bones beneath the clay. I could only imagine her as she was, alive but far away in some heaven beyond my ken.

I suppose heaven is usually a word associated with people who are happy, people who are infused with joy. I remember being at a music gig one time in Omagh. There were men on the stage with banjos, accordions and guitars, and then a woman came out, like a lamb, and folded herself around a bodhrán and I thought for a moment she was going to fall asleep. But all of a sudden it was as if someone had plugged her in, as if electricity was running through her body. The songs possessed her. Although it was her toes, curled up under the chair, that caught my attention, and the sense that something invisible was inhabiting her body and releasing the song. She is in heaven, I thought, as the music flowed through her.

Long ago when I was eating chicken soup at the kitchen table in Cavan my mother would often seem to be in heaven. She would sometimes look at her bowl of broth and say, 'This soup is going down to my toes.'

It was her way of describing the effects of good soup. But when I was at the music gig in Omagh I thought that maybe the songs were having the same effect on the singer because, while she sang, her toes curled up and tapped the floor with a dainty but intense energy, as if the invisible world was bursting through her skin.

My mother danced well. She squeezed her exuberance for life out through her toes onto the floor of the town hall in Cavan, dancing with men who reminded her of Fred Astaire; that was until my father came along and seduced her with so much romantic blather that she was blinded to the fact that he danced like a donkey. And I like to think of her still dancing in some ballroom of bliss or whatever heavenly realm she dissolved into.

And who is to say that my great-grandmother was not like all the rest of us. So I closed my eyes to concentrate for a moment and imagine her smiling at me from far away and the sexton, who may have thought I was saying a prayer, stepped a little bit away to afford me more privacy in that moment.

46

When my father died in 1976, I brought my mother back to the hotel in Cork where she once worked, on a holiday, and the hotel manager she had worked with just happened to be in the building while we were at lunch, although he was retired by then. He came to our table to shake the widow's hand, and my mother flushed with the pleasure of seeing him. In fact, she enjoyed our little holiday so much that I could never again walk in the door of that hotel without thinking about her.

I'm not sure what inspired me to take the beloved there, years later. It was soon after we had begun our love affair. I booked a big room with a Jacuzzi bath and an enormous bed. We scrubbed ourselves in the Jacuzzi and ate big steaks in the dining room and downed a bottle of wine and then went to bed as happy as well-fed cats. But in the middle of the night, I became agitated.

I was flailing about in my sleep and talking babble. She woke me and said, 'You're a hard man to sleep with sometimes.'

I didn't reply because I couldn't think of anything to say. I just gazed at her from my side of the large bed, and after a while she said, 'What are you looking at?'

I didn't have a reply for that but gradually we began to smile.

We gazed a lot at each other in those years, like we were fascinated with the novelty of each other's faces. Nowadays, the only thing we gaze at is the television screen, which I suppose is a kind of outwards-into-the-universe gazing. And when my beloved went away initially, I glued myself to the television. But then I got tired of it. The news didn't seem quite as interesting without her beside me. And I had little else to look at except perhaps the pictures on the wall or the computer screen.

Skype or FaceTime were handy enough. I thought they would keep us connected, satisfy my conversational needs and sustain our intimacy. But in the end I got bored with it. It was only an image on a computer screen. It's not like she was in the room. She wasn't. She was in Warsaw.

In fact, I couldn't even say if she was in Warsaw. At least not based on the grainy, pixelated image on the screen.

For all I knew, she might have been wandering in Ukraine or cloistered in a monastery in Minsk and was refusing to tell me. All she ever said was that she was working with an

48

icon. Some famous image of the Mother of God that was enclosed in a room where she spent her hours with white gloves and the medieval tools of the icon-maker's trade.

But I did sustain myself for a while with the computer screen – particularly on Periscope, an app used by young people all over the world to broadcast live images and receive texts from those who choose to watch. It's a cross between a video and a selfie, and the narcissistic loneliness of young people in various trailer parks and apartment blocks from Los Angeles to Kiev astonished me at first, as they smoked weed and talked about their nail polish. Periscope seemed to allow the loneliest, most solitary child in the world to broadcast their broken heart in public, even if the public was only half a dozen curious others who logged on.

'You think that thing is going to make you happy?' my great-grandmother asked one night.

'What thing?' I wondered.

'That internet thing,' she said. 'If I was you, I'd be very careful of that.'

By now, I was calling her Martha. She was just a photograph but we had become conversational friends, especially when I was halfway down the bottle.

'Don't you worry,' I said with confidence. 'I can control the internet. Besides, what would you know about it?'

'I only want you to be happy,' she said. 'I don't want you

to be depressed. That's why I'm talking to you. And that internet will depress you. Staring at other people's lives will fill your heart with misery. Just turn it off.'

I assured her that I was happy. Or at least not in danger of falling into depression.

'When my beloved returns and the fields are white with daisies, I will light a fire for her, and when the train arrives I will be there to meet her, and we will sit in silence until the fire goes out and we fall asleep – each of us again in the other's shadow.'

50   'Oh dear,' my great-grandmother sighed, 'is that what you think?'

Bucharest

A few days after finding Martha's grave in Dublin, I began to dream of another kind of heaven. Being bored in Leitrim through a long, wet autumn, I had developed a desire to travel somewhere. Anywhere. I knew from experience that the road out of darkness, the path to bliss, is often by way of Dublin airport.

So I went on the internet and bought a ticket to Bucharest for January. Bucharest in the snow would be heaven for a writer, I thought.

When my beloved asked me the following day why I was going to Romania, I said that the ticket was very cheap, I needed a break to write in solitude and there would be a lot of snow. I suppose I didn't want to say that I had been drinking and it's always a bad idea to go on a Ryanair site if you've had too much wine. You never know where you might end up.

Maybe I was jealous of my beloved's adventure in Poland,

coming and going every few months as she furthered her study and exhibited her artwork in various centres around Warsaw. If she can go away on big adventures, I thought, then why can't I? And since I was too proud to follow her to Warsaw, I decided to go somewhere else. Even if it was just for two weeks.

So I booked an apartment in Bucharest for a fortnight, beginning on 7 January and, after a few hours, I got an email from Airbnb confirming the booking. Then a few days later, I got another email from the vendor himself.

54 'Thank you for booking one of our apartments. I am writing to confirm the booking. I read that you are interested in the bicycle as well, so I will book it for you. Do you have WhatsApp?'

All that seemed very good and very professional and then there was a final note which I was over the moon about.

'I have an issue with the flat you booked so I will offer you in the same price a much nicer apartment also downtown.'

Well, I couldn't believe my luck. He was giving me an upgrade.

Below the text, the sender had inserted pictures of the upgrade. It was musty looking. The sofa was enormous. The wireless was like one I remember as a child in our dining room. There were pelmets with tassels above the green curtains. It was all tatty in a luxurious kind of way and had probably been a very deluxe abode in 1950 or whenever they first installed the sofa and fitted the curtains.

But it was swanky and spacious and I didn't really notice that it was in a time warp. Or that, from then on, I was no longer dealing with the vendor through Airbnb but with a private individual, and we were communicating through private emails on a one-to-one basis. I was dealing with a stranger in Bucharest whom I didn't know.

'Yes, I am happy to change to the apartment you described,' I replied after seeing the pictures. 'And, no, I won't need a bicycle.'

(Although I thought it was odd of him to offer one. Considering the temperatures in Bucharest in January, I was hardly going to venture out on a pushbike.) 55

'It's partly a business trip,' I explained. 'I will be doing a lot of writing.'

He replied within the hour.

'So good to hear from you. It will be a rare pleasure to meet. I always love editing and writing articles. Thank you for staying in one of my apartments.'

This was great. His name was Dragos and when I was offline I made up conversations with him. We were like old friends. And what a lovely coincidence that Dragos was also a writer. Or that he liked writing. I imagined he was perhaps working for a large real-estate company who managed exclusive apartments and maybe in his spare time he did a little tinkering with the prospect of being a journalist. Who knows?

He certainly looked like an idealistic young man in the

photograph he sent me. He had dark eyebrows and the innocent, smiling face of an angel in a white shirt as he glanced at the camera. It didn't dawn on me that Dragos could have sent someone else's photograph. Dragos could have been an elderly taxi driver with tattoos or a woman who ran a grocery shop – and Dragos might not even be his name. The photograph proved nothing.

But the emails were impressive and I was willing to be deluded. After a few days, Dragos began using the word 'sir' a lot. I found it very flattering.

56 'Sir, as your trip to Romania is coming soon, I am reaching you to arrange for your check-in. Do you come by plane, sir? Would you like me to arrange airport shuttle for you, sir? I can have my driver to come pick you up from the airport, sir.'

Well, clearly this was a man working with hundreds of clients, from America and Britain and France and all over the world. This was a young man arranging exclusive accommodation for the top brass who did business in Bucharest and I had just by good fortune fallen into his lap. It crossed my mind that he may have procured more than bicycles for his guests. His apartments in the centre of sophisticated Bucharest might possibly be places where men met women. Where businessmen were facilitated in all manners of relaxation.

'Don't even think about it,' Martha said from the wall.

'I had no intention of thinking about it,' I replied. My

lust for other bodies had almost petered out. I imagined Bucharest as a spiritual adventure, a moment of epiphany, of self-realisation in the snow, rather than a wild party of bonking with strange women from the mountains of Transylvania.

Incense burning before an icon in some Orthodox church was my dream of sensual pleasure as I tried to reawaken my slumbering religious faith.

As I had been saying to Martha in the evenings, when we sat together at the fire, all three of us: my beloved at the writing desk, studying the medieval icons of Belarus, and me by the stove, admiring the flames behind the glass of the stove door and sometimes secretly admiring the reflection of fire in Martha's eyes.

'Don't go to Romania,' her eyes were saying. 'It won't do you any good.'

'But what else am I supposed to do?' I wondered.

The beloved turned her head and looked at me.

'Did you say something?'

'Me? No.'

I certainly wasn't going to take the General's advice. I'm not a dog on the porch who buck-leps into the night every chance he gets. Besides, the last dalliance I had of that sort turned out to be a total disaster.

A couple of years ago, a friend I had not seen since we

were students phoned me. The beloved happened to be away. My old friend was a dancer. And the thought of a ballerina in Mayo excited me to extremities. A woman who dances more beautifully than the moon's reflection on water. A soul alive in human form. And she rings me?

'Where are you now?' I asked.

'Ballina,' she said. 'Where are you?'

'Not far away,' I lied.

'I'm working until 5 p.m.,' she said.

I lay on the couch to calm down. The beloved at the time was in Dublin for the weekend with relations.

I was too excited to doze. I just lay there thinking about bills I needed to pay, and the direct debits that were out of control, and the price of hotels in Ballina.

I had two choices. Either book a hotel immediately or wash the dishes. So I washed the dishes. I don't like using the dishwasher, so I washed each thing carefully and slowly, taking it as a practice to enter into the present moment and abandon the carnal and adolescent desires that had got out of control for the few moments I'd been on the phone. But, when I was done, I still wanted to book the hotel. So I cut my toenails. That was a practice through which I could reflect on the ageing and unattractive body I now possessed. Although it could also be a sensible preparation if intimacy with a ballerina was remotely on the cards for later in the evening.

By the time I was finished the toes and had scooped up

the dead nails into an old newspaper it was time to google hotels. Ballina. And up came a new Ramada with balconies and views of the river and spa baths in every room. I didn't know there was a new Ramada in Ballina but it seemed so perfect that I booked it immediately and when the ballerina phoned and said she had finished work I said I'd be in Mayo in two hours.

'Where will we meet?' she wondered.

'The Ramada,' I suggested. 'They have three restaurants.'

Of course I didn't mention the room. I said, 'I'll text you the location.'

And I did. I texted the hotel link and she phoned back and said, 'I don't think this is such a good idea.'

'Why not?' I wondered.

'Well,' she said, 'that hotel is in Australia.'

She added that she was only thinking of a quick coffee before she got the bus for Dublin. Her tone was flat and lifeless, and all hope of a romantic evening withered.

Bucharest would be different. I didn't know how many travellers or visitors Dragos had dealt with, or what limits he'd set on the services he'd provide for them, but that didn't bother me. Who cared if he kept his guests happy with pleasures and services of a carnal nature? Who cared if he employed poor girls from remote regions of the Carpathian valley to provide exotic services? I was on a different mission. To find heaven. Avoid depression. Get out of the winter rain. And stop being jealous of the beloved because she was coming and going to Warsaw.

I imagined Dragos had dozens of uniformed chauffeurs with fancy cars at the airport on any night of the week.

'So, yes,' I emailed him, 'I will be glad to take a shuttle. Will it cost much?'

'For you,' he replied, 'the transport will be a gift from us. Because we always appreciate very nice people like you coming to stay at our apartments.'

60 Maybe he'd seen *Riverdance*. Maybe he really liked Irish people.

'Also let me know if you have any preference for drinks. Soda. Ice. Water: sparkling or non. Coffee: normal or decaf.'

'I'll miss you,' the beloved said.

'But I miss you too,' I replied, 'when you're away in Warsaw.' This was tit for tat.

I was really looking forward to meeting Dragos. And I told him so in a final email on the day before the flight.

Dragos emailed back that 'unfortunately I will be in Barcelona until 30 January'.

Which was, coincidentally, the day after my planned departure from Bucharest.

'But my colleague Mrs Adriana will be there if you need anything.'

It was a nice name. Adriana. So I emailed him like I would a friend. I said I was sorry to miss him. I thanked him for the complimentary transportation and said that I drank sparkling water and normal coffee.

My beloved left me at the airport on the morning of the flight. I kissed her goodbye. She smiled and said, 'I hope you have a great time.'

And I went through the boarding gate and survived the din of security men with loud Dublin voices shouting at the passengers to take out their laptops and take off their shoes, and I sat in a restaurant drinking coffee and I checked my email for the last time and sure enough there was a new message in my inbox from Dragos.

'Hey,' Dragos wrote, 'I just confirmed that my office has all chauffeurs busy for this evening. So I am sending you with my personal driver. He will be there to pick you up at 20.35 at the airport in arrivals, next to Segafredo coffee boutique.'

Great, I thought. No confusions.

Who could ask for more? And the forecast was for snow all that week. Lots of snow and freezing temperatures. Below −3. It was going to be so wonderful, walking about the streets under the blue sky and watching blizzards from my cosy sofa.

I would be in heaven, as they say. Walking through the snow in silence to some ancient church where an icon hung silently in the shadows.

This is what I needed. It wasn't much to expect. A quiet moment. Just to pull myself together. And, afterwards, I would find a café on a cobbled street and sip tea and wait for stories to fall into my lap.

I've always loved Romania. When I was studying theology in Maynooth in the early 1980s, there had been two monks in my class who had come from an Orthodox monastery in the Carpathian valley. They wore traditional black robes and headpieces, and they had long black beards and blessed themselves with great reverence as they gazed with beautiful brown eyes towards the tabernacle.

In the winter of 1982, I was an ordained priest, studying for a Higher Diploma in Education. On 7 January, it snowed along the east of the country and the earth was covered in deep frozen waves of snow, drifts so deep that the silence covered my anxieties, and the snow lay for a very long time because no traffic could move and everyone was stranded in the place they had been on the first evening of that great falling.

I was in my room in Dunboyne House. It was the tail end of the Christmas holiday and most other students were absent but I had gone back to finish an essay that was almost a month overdue. As I looked out the window of my bedroom on the third floor, at the trees and shrubs whitening in the quad, I saw the two monks from Romania in their skirts playing with the snow and dancing like children. Clearly, they had made the right choice when they became monks, because they were happy.

Maybe a life of solitude and devotion to God was really a good idea, I thought, if it generated in those beautiful young men the spontaneity and joy that was visible in the snow. Unless they were bipolar.

64 I often suspected that young men who practised chastity might suffer from extremes of elation and depression. The cloisters suited them because the grim silence of God suits the melancholic heart, and chastity practised by young people can induce over-exuberance, great excesses of sudden inexplicable joy, like geysers of boiling steam rising up through the frozen ice. I suspected even back then that my own attraction to religious life was not unassociated with my alternate bouts of melancholy and elation.

When I was a child, I used to believe deeply that my guardian angel held my hand when I slept, and I thought that snowflakes were angels' feathers falling from heaven. I told this to a teacher once, but the teacher scoffed at me and asked how did I think wet snowflakes could be feathers.

'Clearly,' the teacher said, 'feathers don't melt.'

'But perhaps they fall through the universe,' I suggested,

'and since the universe is very cold they might change to ice on the way.'

The teacher wasn't amused.

'The flakes come from the clouds,' he said.

But for years, even in adulthood, I thought of angels every time I saw snow on the roof of a house or the bonnet of a car.

Of course I couldn't tell anyone that I believed in angels or that sometimes in winter as the snow fell, I would feel myself blessed as I walked through it, shaking the white tufts from my boots.

My therapist would never sanction any form of religious talk.

'It's just the child inside you,' she would say, 'trying to feel secure. Hoping to be mothered.'

'So what do I do?' I wondered.

'Well,' she said, 'when the child feels frightened, you must hold him and tell him there is no need to be afraid anymore.'

'How can I hold the child if he's inside me?' I asked.

'Use a cushion,' the therapist said. 'Talk to the cushion as if it were the child that you used to be.'

I found that helpful enough and not at all difficult, except when other people were around the house – I didn't want visitors to catch me talking to the furnishings.

I couldn't believe my good fortune: to be stranded in the college with two monks in the middle of a snowstorm. There was no sign of professors in the corridors. The refectory was silent. The Christmas decorations still hung on a tree in the main cloister, but the only people in the world as far as I was concerned were myself and the two monks.

I knocked on their door and they welcomed me and offered tea. They had two single rooms on the floor below me, but they spent a lot of time together in one or other room. A small lamp glowed in the corner and, behind it, was an icon propped against the wall. Mary the Mother, sorrowful and silent, her face enveloped in a golden halo.

66

We became friends quickly and every morning for a week, I worked on my essay and then rushed down to their rooms. We walked in the snow, discussed God and drank in the student pub, where they had fruit juices and, on the way home one night, their black beards were tinged with frost, and the world was so dark and white that I felt as if I was walking around in a Russian novel. They invited me in for tea and we sat in silence before the icon.

Their rooms were clean and tidy and the icon of Mary was always a living presence in the corner. The lamp burned constantly, even when they went out. Whenever we walked across the quad in the snow, we could see the flickering light on the wall through the window. Gradually, the icon grew in my heart like a fire in the snow.

But the trip to Romania in 2015 was a disaster. Even before
the plane landed I was stressed out. I got a headache on
the flight. I had paid for a seat near the door, but it was
colder than I expected at forty thousand feet. When we
landed there was a shuttle bus on the apron to take us to
the terminal. Everything around was white. The passengers
in cheap plastic anoraks were perished and little clouds of
fog emerged from their mouths as they walked.

They all had brown eyes. A fact which awakened in me
some deeply buried fear.

When I got as far as Segafredo café in the corner of the
arrivals lobby I ordered a coffee and waited at a round table
for Marius, my chauffeur, to arrive. I imagined someone
in a peaked cap, a grey uniform, perhaps, with my name
written on a cardboard placard. But there was no Marius
and no uniform.

When he did turn up, an hour later, he was toothless,

unshaven and looked like he might have been sleeping rough for most of the winter.

I didn't know who the stranger at the door staring at me was. I finished my second coffee and clutched my bags beneath the table, hoping he wasn't going to approach and beg for money.

When he did come, gingerly he took out a cigarette packet from his coat and placed it on the table. My name was scrawled on the back.

'Are you Marius?' I asked in astonishment.

He nodded and I nodded and with the restraint of strangers meeting on neutral territory we smiled, and then he walked me outside into the freezing car park.

Marius had a Toyota Corolla, very bashed up on the passenger side so that the front passenger door didn't open. He negotiated me into the back seat and we drove to the city with one headlamp. There were three coats on the back seat and I remembered again that my email exchanges had been with a person I'd never met, and one of these greasy black coats on the back seat might well belong to Dragos, or indeed this stranger who was driving me into town with one headlamp. Indeed Marius might be Dragos. We travelled through the night towards the centre of town, across wide junctions with many lanes and lots of traffic lights though there were no other cars moving. We drove sometimes down small side streets and into little alleyways and I was about to jump out screaming in terror that we were going to end up at the door of some seedy place where men watched snuff movies. But just as we slowed down in a narrow street of red neon, we turned the corner and emerged from the alley into the main city streets again.

Marius smoked as he drove, lighting a second cigarette from the butt of the first and throwing the butt out the window into the freezing fog. He eyed me in the mirror as if he knew what I was thinking. Maybe he does this every Saturday night, I thought. Maybe he was the driver that transported the sacrificial flesh. Maybe there was a constant stream of sheep that came on flights from Western Europe to be fleeced in the side streets, their credit cards tapped for thousands of euros before the owners were disposed of.

Would they just force me to push my card into an ATM in the wall and then tell me to walk home? Or would they slice me up as meat to feed guard dogs later in the night?

It's funny how racism becomes the embodiment of fear when we are under threat. I had no reason to believe that Marius was anything but an honest, poor man working for small money, driving a taxi.

And while I felt waves of fear and prejudice in one moment, I also felt overcome by moments of shame for having such thoughts. And I tried to catch his eye in the rear-view mirror and smile. But he didn't smile back.

Just after a roundabout in the city centre, we pulled over

to the kerb on a wide street. The car heaved up onto the snow like a boat hitting dry land and he stepped into the freezing fog to make a phone call.

I too decided to use my phone.

'Jesus,' the beloved exclaimed when she heard my voice. 'Is everything OK?'

'Fine.'

'Have you landed?'

'Yes. I'm just in a taxi waiting to find my apartment.'

'Lucky you. Is it cold?'

'Yes,' I said, 'it looks cold outside. But the taxi is warm.' And I fondled one of the three old coats on the back seat.

'So why are you ringing?'

'No reason. Just bored here. Waiting for someone to come and bring me to the apartment.'

I hoped my GPS coordinates would lodge in her phone's memory so that if something happened to me later, someone could trace this call. If it was my last call before I vanished off the face of the earth, then at least they could track where the body might be. But I said none of this. I didn't want to frighten her. And then I told her that I had to hang up because I could see the woman coming.

Mrs Adriana was wearing tight denim jeans, black leather boots and a furry hooded anorak as she walked up to Marius, a little brown dog on a leash barked at her heels. She paid Marius in notes and then poked her face in the window. She smelled lovely, and the world seemed normal again.

I followed her around the corner towards a block of flats and across various slippy pathways where the snow had been pushed into heaps and turned to ice. Eventually we arrived at our destination: an apartment block built in the 1950s with solid concrete, and heavy steel doors, and a concrete stairwell.

I followed her to the second floor where she knocked at a door that an old lady then opened. I could smell cabbage.

The old lady had a huge lower lip and a pink tongue that hung out when she smiled. And she did smile but it was very toothy so I wasn't sure if she liked me or wanted to eat me.

Just inside on the left, there was a dining area and a television set, and on the right there were two further doors with foggy glass panelling. I guessed one was a toilet and one a bedroom.

But at the far end of the space there was another door. Mrs Adriana took a bunch of keys from her lambskin coat and opened this door to reveal the apartment I had seen in Dragos' emails.

And it was impressive. There were two big brown armchairs and a sofa. The kitchen glistened with chrome and steel. Dinner plates, wine glasses and a coffee percolator sat on a white Ikea worktop. There were knives and forks in the drawers and two oranges lay in a basket on the worktop. At the far end of the hallway, there was a bathroom. And while the kitchen and hallway looked like they had been built yesterday, the sitting room, bedroom and bathroom might have been there since the time of Stalin. I had seen it all on the internet, though no one had mentioned that the apartment had no separate entrance, that it was part of some old lady's home. Nor had the internet revealed the constant hissing noise that came from the radiators.

The shower curtain in the bathroom was torn. There was no water in the bathroom taps, and the radiators were broken. But I didn't despair immediately. I could see snow on the streets outside and the cross of an Orthodox church in the distance. Those were signs. The cross and the church and a layer of snow were enough for me to risk it.

Mrs Adriana didn't waste words. She didn't explain how anything worked or why I was in someone else's apartment. She gave me keys and showed me how to open the door from the street and then get into my apartment, and then she left without as much as a smile or handshake.

I searched for bedclothes, but found only three thin blankets, an eiderdown and a single nylon sheet. I checked the radiators. Sometimes one of them heated up for a while and then hissed and went cold. I hadn't even taken off my coat. I sat on the sofa wondering if I would freeze in the night and die alone.

My darkest fantasies about Dragos returned. Perhaps he intended to strap me to the sofa and cut my throat and make a snuff movie about an Irishman bleeding to death. Or maybe he would strip me naked and leave me chained to the radiator without water until I died.

At least through my beloved's phone records, they would find my body. I could be taken home and buried with dignity.

Eventually, I lay down in my overcoat, beneath the blankets and the thin duvet, and slept. And the following day I felt much better.

73

I sat on the sofa eating an orange, remembering a day Steve Wickham had come to my house, a beautiful musician with long black hair and a precious fiddle. He had come to the door, up the hill through the fog. He'd stepped into the room and opened the fiddle case and took the instrument from the blue silk scarf he always wrapped around it. He'd leaned his chin on the fiddle so that his long hair fell over his cheeks and then he pulled the bow across the low strings, bleeding a deep sound out of them, like a shaman opening a door to the other world.

Between tunes, he sat lazily waiting for more tunes to arrive. Music teaches a simple lesson. Wait for the tune. Play the tune. Be present in every moment. That seemed clearer than anything I ever found in the libraries of religion or philosophy.

So I searched for Steve Wickham in my music library

and, as his tunes flowed from the computer, I visualised him sitting beside me. 'Don't be afraid,' he said.

Later, I walked the slushy streets and the iced-up pavements, ate a fine breakfast in a nearby diner, tried to be chirpy in simple English and kept stressing to people that I was Irish in case they thought me English. That's just one more complex I suffer from.

A waiter stared at me as if I were an elephant. But I didn't care.

I sat on the musty sofa that evening listening to more music and to the sound of traffic outside in the dark. Even the lack of water for a bath didn't bother me. I was settling in.

I began to visit churches. To sneak in and out. To mimic the devotion of others as they made the sign of the cross. To stand just inside the door, gazing at the icons above the sanctuary lamp. The wall of icons that hid the altar. And the child inside me said, 'This is the real presence. I am not alone here.'

But, in truth, I was frightened. And I was alone. I was frightened of the dog that patrolled the apartment through which I was required to walk whenever I entered or left my section. It crossed my mind that if the woman outside my door stuck her key into the lock and turn it then I would be a prisoner. And even if someone came from the

Irish embassy enquiring, she could stand at her front door and say she never knew me, and they could not prove her wrong.

It was all paranoia, and it all hinged on there being something slightly sinister about Dragos. He was a stranger to me and into that word, as if it were an empty vessel, I poured all my racist poison and childish fears. Dragos had become my enemy.

So there I stood one afternoon, in mid-January 2015, in a doorway of an Orthodox church in Bucharest, and I looked up at the sky and realised that the first snow of the afternoon was about to fall. I could see the first flakes coming towards me. I stood waiting until it was a full flurry and then I stood waiting for it to end.

There was a young couple sheltering in the porch beside me and they looked almost surprised to be alive. They too were watching the snow. And their eyes followed the flakes and they laughed.

The young couple were amazed with the snow but I thought that they were probably amazed with each other. And because there were books in their backpacks, I presumed that they might be students. I wanted to go over to them and say, 'You are really a lovely couple.' But I didn't because I wasn't that mad.

My student life began in 1971, I used to drink hot whiskeys in the Roost, a pub in Maynooth, with an American girlfriend, through another long winter of unusually heavy snow. And we would make a song and dance about it, going back up the slushy street to our flat just beside the Leinster Arms, a flat which I shared with two other male students who also had lovers who slept over on Friday nights. We would drink wine and cider from white plastic cups all through the night and recite poems about snow or winter or love from various anthologies that were on our English courses. It was a kind of quiz.

Each in turn would ask, 'Who wrote this?' before reciting a particular poem. The rest then had to guess the author.   77

My girlfriend got the identity of the poet right almost fifty per cent of the time until eventually one of the other boys exclaimed, 'You're some cunt!'

The exclamation implied that he was positively impressed by her erudition but to her young American ears she could not have been more disgusted if he had vomited green bile and spun his head around 360 degrees.

I tried to explain that Irish people sometimes used the word in conversation as a form of affection or admiration.

'For example,' I continued, 'if a farmer in Cavan grows excessively large and beautiful cabbages his neighbours might likely remark that those cabbages are serious cunts.'

But she wasn't amused and she stormed out and I had to go after her. We were on the street in the yellow glow of a street lamp and I was pleading for her to come back inside, when all of a sudden she turned her head to the sky and said, 'Look!'

And I looked up and saw the first snow descending.

'Angels,' I whispered, though I was a grown man. She kissed me suddenly on the lips and said, 'Happy Christmas.'

As if the snow changed everything. As if flakes were angels who could hold us and wipe away all our bad feelings.

And so years later, on the street in Bucharest, I had an urge to walk up to the young couple in the porch of the church and wish them a happy new year. But I didn't have sufficient Romanian to do that. And, besides, it was already the middle of January and Christmas was over. All I could do was go home to the apartment and talk to the cushion on the sofa.

78

On the third night, the heating went off completely and the temperature outside dropped below –3°C.

I drank vodka and blackcurrant juice for a few hours to keep warm and tried to contact the beloved by Skype and Facebook and on her mobile phone. But no luck. I tried my daughter but she was elsewhere too.

When I woke up the following morning, the Charlie Hebdo massacre was all over the news, the internet and Facebook.

The world was falling apart. A text from the beloved asked: 'Were you looking for me?'

'No,' I replied. 'All great here.'

A few moments later, I had second thoughts, and knowing she was now at home I tried to get her on Skype. But the internet connection had died while I was pouring boiling water on a camomile teabag. I felt totally fucked.

Game set and match to Dragos.

I walked out into the white streets where the snow was beginning to melt. I was looking for breakfast.

In the café on the corner, a waiter was standing at the reception desk, his elbow leaning against the counter and his head twisted to follow the news on the television. He had a pot of tea in his hand but he was transfixed as he gazed at the images of the massacre in France.

'I have a brother in Paris,' he said when he was bringing my omelette and thin slivers of bacon.

People looked at me as if I were as insignificant as a stray cat. I was dissolving into Romania, turning numb from fear and anxiety. Soon, I would be invisible to myself. I would no longer recognise my own voice. I would look in the mirror and be unable to act. And then Dragos would come, in through the window with big teeth and skin me alive. And though the lady in the flat might not be dangerous, who is to say that her son would not come some day and that he would look at me without pity.

'Today you don't go out,' he might say. 'Today you stay in.'

When I got back to the apartment, I texted Dragos: 'You must get the radiators working immediately.'

Dragos replied instantly saying that he was still in Barcelona. He said he would get Mrs Adriana to phone.

After a few moments, the same number showed up again on my screen, this time as an incoming call.

'Hello,' Mrs Adriana said. 'Dragos tell me you have problem with heating.'

Could Mrs Adriana be Dragos? I wondered.

'Can you fix it?' I asked.

'It will be Monday,' she said.

After that I turned to the internet to find flights to Dublin, but tragically the internet was down again. I stood up and wandered around the apartment, staring into the mirror at the door and the mirror over the mantelpiece and the mirror in the bathroom, saying over and over again, 'I'm fucked. I'm really fucked.'

I tried the phone once again and once again I got Mrs Adriana's sweet little voice. 'Hi,' she said, like she was just about to stick her tongue in my ear.

'Hi,' I replied, sweet as I could too, like maybe I was really looking forward to her tongue in my ear.

She said, 'Hi,' again, really calm and relaxed – she must have thought I was beginning to chill.

But then I lost it.

'Now fuck this, Mrs Adriana!' I said. 'This is not acceptable. You need to get over here and I'm going to let you keep the money for the first week and you will give me back the money I paid you for the second week because I'm going home. I'm leaving. I'm a very important person. You don't even know who I am. I could be a film-maker and I just got a call from my people and I have to get a plane home immediately.'

There was a long silence on the line.

'You make films?' she asked.

I decided to hang up. I had done the deed. The words had come out in the correct order.

To be fair to Mrs Adriana, she came over in a cloud of
perfume, all booted up in leather and fur, within half an
hour.

She smiled at me and said, 'You make films?'

And if she had confessed that her middle name was
Dragos, I would have embraced her and asked if I could
stay for the month.

But she didn't.

'What kind of films you make?'

I had no answer. And she must have figured out I was
lying because she turned sour and then she counted out my
money in a surly manner, and thanked me and said to leave
the key on the table when I was leaving.

That afternoon, I fled with my little wheelie case and
found a hotel just two blocks away without the slightest
bother. I checked into a room with a bath en suite, a warm
bed, two clean duvets and a leaflet beside the phone with

taxi numbers and details in English about travelling to the airport.

I soaked in the bath and lay on the bed watching Romanian television news and then slept until morning, when I linked my laptop to the Wi-Fi and got into another hot bath as Charlie McGettigan spoke to Miriam O'Callaghan on Irish radio about the Eurovision Song Contest. It felt like being back in the hills above Lough Allen. Another simple Sunday morning.

The radio reception was so good that I might as well have been in the Jacuzzi with the pair of them, Charlie and Miriam. The power of the internet to banish the blues delighted me and I had no further bouts of anxiety from then until my bags were packed, my taxi had taken me to the airport, my boarding card was checked and I sat in the front seat of a Ryanair flight to Dublin.

It was late when I arrived home from Bucharest. I lit the stove, turned on the television and sat passively through a show called *The Meaning of Life* in which Gay Byrne interrogated famous people about their idea of heaven.

There was no sign of the beloved, but what can I say. Was she in SuperValu? Was she in Warsaw?

No. As it turned out she was visiting a neighbour in hospital and wasn't back until midnight. She found me on the sofa staring at a blue screen on the TV.

'What are you watching?' she asked. A troublesome question since the screen was blank. Although it didn't remain blank for long. She asked me if I wanted to talk about the trip but I was too upset to discuss the mess I'd made so we opened a bottle of wine and watched the first episode of *House of Cards* before we went to bed.

In fact, we mopped up loads of episodes during January, until the stillness of Mrs Underwood, the ice queen, and her bloodthirsty, deranged husband bored us into an alcoholic haze. They were too clear and beautiful and ambitious for us. We were not like them.

'I thought you had planned to be in Warsaw after Christmas?' I said.

'Not until February,' she replied. 'The academy is closed for some reason. So I'll be here until the end of the month.'

When darkness closed in the following evening, we rummaged through shelves of DVDs until we found the box set of *Shoah*, a documentary about the Holocaust and its aftermath in Poland. We had done this before, as a ritual, during the winter. Sitting together, holding hands, bearing witness to the atrocities of history. We watched for a week, one hour a night, never commenting or speaking about it.

It wasn't entertainment. It was a religious act. To view *Shoah* is like a session of analytic meditation. We just did it. Watched it. Witnessed the story. Acknowledged its truth.

And by the end of January, the beloved was packing her bags again. She had a three-month residency in Warsaw and two sculptural exhibitions to prepare for.

'Will you come to the opening in April?' she asked.

I couldn't.

'I have a tour lined up,' I explained. 'And then an acting gig in Dublin.'

At the end of January, I drove her to the airport at 4 a.m. so that she could get the plane at 9.30 a.m. Our lips touched lightly in the car park. I walked her to the boarding gate. Our lips repeated the gesture of a kiss. And she was gone.

I drove back to the hills above Lough Allen. *Shoah*, the box set of footage from the darkest moment in European history, lay on the floor under the television table. My Polish great-grandmother looked at me from the wall.

Crows in Kilkenny

The reading tour I began in February 2015 took me from Kerry to Donegal and from Dublin to Galway, covering over thirty venues. Sometimes, on my way to a venue, I'd meet a stranger in a café or at the deli in a filling station or even along the road, and we'd get into playful conversation.

In Galway one morning, I was having a breakfast of poached eggs and toast not far from Eyre Square. A big old man came in and started counting his money at the table in front of me. He was making sure he had the price of his tea before he went to the counter.

'I'm sorry,' he said. 'I'll be out of your way in a moment.' His face was weather-beaten and his hands were huge.

'You're not in my way at all,' I said.

My accent caught his attention.

'Where are you from?' he enquired.

'Cavan,' I said.

'Oh,' he exclaimed, 'Ray Carolan. The footballer.'

'Yes,' I said, 'I know the name.'

'I knew him years ago,' he said

'Where are you from?' I enquired.

'Connemara,' he replied.

Though he looked like he was over seventy, he was lean and agile and was wearing a tracksuit and runners.

'You're a fit man,' I said. 'Did you play football?'

'I played everything,' he said. 'And I boxed and I did two marathons.'

'Did you know the famous Thornton in Connemara?' I asked, referring to a well-known boxer long ago.

'I knew him well,' he said. 'I used to talk to him.'

Thus we had established a connection. Where are you from? And do I know someone you know? And off we went over poached eggs and rashers and mugs of tea, talking like two kings about the universe.

Stories would follow, random and intimate, and that gave me material to write about or talk about onstage.

Sometimes, it was in the most unlikely places that I was ambushed by a stranger and entangled in wonderful conversation.

I was driving in a lonely part of County Laois one day, heading for the Dunamaise Arts Centre in Portlaoise, when I met a woman in wellingtons and a man's coat, following cattle on the roadway. I slowed down and opened the window and said hello.

She said her maiden name and her married name were the same. 'And if two people with the same name marry and make brown bread,' she said, 'then they will have the cure of the whooping cough.'

I said, 'I once knew a man called Grey who married a woman called White. Do you think,' I enquired, 'that there might be cures associated with one colour marrying another?'

By this stage, we were getting on so well that I was worried her husband might come out of some gap in the ditch and ask me awkward questions.

93

The cattle were dripping dung from their rear ends, but the road was narrow and there was no point in stressing them by driving through so I cruised along beside the woman and we continued chatting.

'My husband is in England,' she said, as if she was reading my mind. 'That's why I'm out trying to gather these cattle.'

I said I was heading for Portlaoise and that I was coming from Stradbally.

'Stradbally's a fine town,' she said.

I said, 'I had a girlfriend once who worked in the stone yard in Stradbally, and, one winter's day many years ago, I hitched from Dublin to visit her. She wanted me to bring her a flask, so she could have some way of keeping her soup warm while she was working.'

'And did you bring her the flask?' the woman of the cowherd asked.

'I did,' I said, 'it was a red flask.'

'And did you hold on to the girl?'

'I did,' I said, 'and I held on to the flask as well.'

'You must be from Cavan so,' she said.

I said, 'How did you know that?' But the cattle were turning in the gate of a large farmyard, and she went after them humming to herself.

94

But although I had fun onstage, telling stories of small anarchies from the highways and byways of the country, I was feeling something different inside. Not depression exactly but a kind of ultimate loneliness that I can only describe with the Gaelic word 'uaigneas'.

It was more disturbing than the dips of depression I had experienced in previous years or the dramatic collapse into melancholy that had paralysed me when I was in my fifties.

This was different. It was like a mortal enemy had arrived. It was the certainty that there are only so many days a human being can remain standing. And the only thing I had as an antidote to that unease was to keep talking, to tell more stories. So it's strange to be onstage acting a comic role, clowning around with the little intimacies of one's private life, listening to the audience laugh, and yet, inside, feeling uneasy and isolated.

'My story is a gift for you,' I whispered to the strangers. 'And your story is my food and drink.'

Off-stage, I had begun to resemble every other ageing male worried about the shortening years ahead. And what disturbed me most was the idea that nothing would remain in my wake. Therefore, it was all meaningless. It would all be forgotten.

In recent years, I'd become sour. I'd become more selfish. I took my beloved for granted. As if she was a given. As if she was a mountain, made for me to look at. And I became short tempered with my daughter if her surf suit was dripping on the bathroom floor where she hung it up to dry.

For no particular reason, I made a copy of Martha's photograph with my phone and used it as a screen wallpaper. I'd look at her bobbing in the phone holder on the dashboard as I drove, wondering if she had brothers or sisters. What was her father like? Did she love her mother? Where in Poland was she born? Did she grow up on a farm? Or have a boyfriend?

Did she get a boat to London? Or Liverpool? Or a train? Was she running from a violent husband? Who came with her? What did she feel when she first saw Dublin from the deck of a steamboat? How did she imagine the universe came into being?

Sometimes I would imagine her in the moments before she put on the dress in the photographic studio. A peasant child from the forest speaking broken English in a London shop, perhaps. Discussing how much the photograph would cost. Dreaming of whom she would send it too.

Surely there must be some trace of her. Some tracks of the animal. Some record about her hidden in the great fold of forgetting. Maybe. Or maybe not.

A story is the most beautiful way of bearing witness to the world. Even lovers are more present to each other when they speak their stories in whispers on the pillow or casually confess their private histories as they busy themselves in the kitchen, caught up in the mundane entanglement of cooking food.

Stories are fun. They complete the impossible conundrum of existence. How could Martha's life have any meaning if there was no story left?

I love the way people speak their stories to strangers. People sit in cafés all across Europe telling their life in stories. They pass the time in refugee camps telling stories. They pull my sleeve on the train and say, 'Listen to me. I could write a book about what happened.'

Sometimes strangers even knock on my door and, when I open it, they're standing with their entire life waiting to be told.

Like one night years ago, when a teenage boy arrived at my house in an old Toyota and announced that he was looking for land to rent.

'My brother has two mares,' he said, 'and he's looking to put them on grass.'

I told him I only had an acre, and it was covered with trees. Then, out of curiosity, I asked him if the horses were piebald, because I've been fond of the piebald ever since I'd first seen Tonto and the Lone Ranger on a neighbour's black-and-white television one wet Saturday afternoon, when I was a child. I didn't quite understand what exactly Tonto and the Lone Ranger did, apart from gallop about on the grainy world of the television screen, but I loved the horses.

I told all this to the boy at the door, who looked very gaunt and desperate, and I shuddered to think what his horses might look like after spending the winter perishing in the rain and being fed buckets of slop from a kitchen in some tiny backyard, as he described it to me.

'Please,' he said, 'you must listen to me. My brother really loves his horses – he loves them horses even more than his car, and he drives a Subaru.'

On the road throughout that spring, I checked into a different hotel every day and ate my midday meal alone. Each afternoon, I went to the venue and checked the sound and lights with the engineer and then retired to the hotel to rest. In the evenings, I sat in the dressing room looking at my face in the mirror, going over a few notes about what to say onstage, putting on a linen suit and waiting for the cue to walk into the lights and meet the public.

My readings were usually about grief, the death of my mother or what men do when they are left alone, and as I drove across the country from Galway to Dún Laoghaire and from Letterkenny to Tralee, the audience's laughter reverberated in my ears. I talked about my mother's sorrow in old age, and the way she sat in her chair eating her dinner alone and growing bitter, and how, after her funeral, I found in her house the tracks of the beautiful woman she once had been, hidden away in old photographs and in boxes of hats that she had worn when she was young.

99

My props onstage consisted of the numerous hats she had acquired in her lifetime, and which I had found after she died, and a suitcase belonging to my father. It sat onstage each night until I opened it and offered the audience comic cameos of my mother in various postures and situations. It was an unusual way to mourn my mother: going around the country recalling humorous anecdotes about her.

Meeting the audience was like therapy. Not for the audience, but for me. It was a personal conversation. I talked onstage, and then afterwards people talked to me. Firstly in the queue that lined up to get books signed. Then in the bar of the hotel, where people might recognise me from earlier and come over to say they were at the show. Or even the following morning, in the breakfast room, when someone who had seen my face on television or on a poster somewhere touched my shoulder as we queued for muesli and a hot breakfast, and said they had read one of my books. It became home, this talking to strangers, and I was happy to talk.

One morning in a Galway hotel, I was in the sauna and the woman beside me was crying. I didn't know her. She was just another member of the leisure centre. But I had never seen anyone crying in the sauna before. The leisure centre was empty except for the two of us, so it didn't matter.

'I can barely get out of bed in the mornings,' she said. 'I don't know why.'

I didn't quite know what to say, but I tried as best I could to sound like a therapist.

'Perhaps you have lost interest in what is on the outside,' I said, 'because you are so unhappy on the inside.'

'Well, I think that's obvious,' she said, and she looked at me as if I was the worst therapist she had ever met, either in or out of a sauna. But at least she had stopped crying. It was a posh hotel. The kind of place where ladies arrive in white Audis because their husbands work with NAMA.

I towelled myself in the changing room and thought the

lady in the sauna might have more to say, so I waited in the lobby and offered to buy her a coffee when she emerged.

'I'm sorry if I sounded a bit silly,' I said. 'I'm not a very good counsellor. Can I get you a coffee?'

She was delighted. I ordered it at reception and then we waited in two big armchairs by the glass wall.

'Do you know,' she said, 'that signing on is the most horrible thing? The shame I feel is terrible. I brought letters in my hand the first morning so that people would think I was only there to post them. But I knew the fellow behind the counter. And he was so shocked to see me signing on that he couldn't count my money straight.'

'So how can you afford to be here,' I wondered, 'if you're on the dole?'

I winced after blurting out the question. But she didn't seem to mind now.

'I got three months' membership as a Christmas gift from a friend,' she explained. 'I was rundown and my friend discovered that there was no nutrition in my blood at all, and she does the Chinese pulses, so she made me up a diet of mung beans, rice and coriander. It feeds the blood. And she booked me in here for three months.'

She asked me why I was chatting her up. I said, 'I'm not chatting you up.'

'So what are you doing?' she wondered as the waiter placed two lattes on the round table.

'I get urges to reach out to people,' I explained. 'I love stories. I always have. Like daffodils pushing their stems up into the air and trying to be born again.'

She seemed confused about the daffodils and slightly uneasy, so I made an effort to be more explicit.

'I'm a writer,' I said, 'and I am touring the country with my book. I visit various arts centres and do readings from the book.'

That worked. She remembered seeing me once on television and we had two more lattes and ended up having a great chat.

On another day, I was stopped at a filling station near Ballinaleck on my way to a gig in Longford when I saw a poster on the glass doors for a family festival in Streete, not far away. There was a concert the following evening in the church and so, after the Longford gig, I doubled back. I knew I'd get oodles of stories at a family festival.

The concert was in a church, but not for any religious reasons. The folk singer, Mary McPartlan, was performing with Rick Epping on concertina and Aiden Brennan on guitar.

The church was still used as a church, and it was strange to see the musicians parked in front of the altar singing pagan songs. When the February night closed in and the spotlights lit up the sanctuary, I felt that the saints standing on their shadowed plinths or gazing out from stained-glass windows seemed strangely aloof and indifferent.

On the wall behind the musicians, there was a crucifix – a wounded, outstretched Jesus in his act of sacrifice, made spooky by the shadows. His head was bowed in despair, and the broken-hearted figure seemed like a perfect icon of human sorrow.

When the gig was over, I followed the audience into a pub, and I met a man with watery eyes standing at the bar with a pint of lager in his fist. I was ordering a drink and as I stood beside him waiting for my pint he told me that he used to listen to Dire Straits albums when he was in the seminary.

'Oh,' I said, 'were you a priest?'

'Yes,' he said, 'but I don't have many funny stories.'

'Why did you leave?' I wondered.

'I got tired,' he replied. 'Closing coffins and shovelling clay into open graves. Because I didn't believe any of it. When I opened the front door of a funeral parlour and saw another family in black coats and suits, I would summon up twaddle about God's will and heavenly peace, though the words stuck in my throat.'

He took a sip of his beer and his face looked like he was drinking vinegar.

'So eventually I left.'

I asked him was he at the music gig in the church.

He wasn't. So I told him that he'd missed a wonderful night's fun. 'McPartlan's voice was exquisite,' I said. 'She's such a good singer.'

But he just grimaced. I suppose all he was bothered listening to was the soundtrack to his own remorse.

That night, I set the alarm on my clock as I normally did in the hotel bedroom. I watched another episode of *The Good Wife*, and then I saw Martha on my phone screen and began worrying if I was perhaps getting a bit too obsessed with this ghostly woman.

Maybe I should never have gone to her grave. Standing over that little mound of earth in Dundrum where she was interred while I was already in a melancholic state had triggered me into a deeper kind of loneliness.

I was in love with a phantom. I was talking to the dead. I looked at her sideways, my head on the pillow, her face on the phone, as she once was, some moment long ago in a photographic studio. I kissed her goodnight. And in the morning she was there again, when the alarm called me to another day, another shower, another dining room of pork sausages, black puddings and freshly poached eggs.

'Maybe I should never have accepted a part in this fucking play,' I said to Martha. 'I'm not an actor. I'm just a storyteller who writes and who performs and who sometimes gets cast in conventional plays. I only said yes because I thought it would be wonderful to collaborate with others and to tell someone else's story.'

But seeing my face on the back of a bus, wearing a peaked cap and a false beard, had alarmed me. The pose in the poster had been modelled on an image of Richard Harris in the movie version of the play. I was almost finished my thirty-venue reading tour and we had not yet begun rehearsals and yet there I was on the bus.

'Holy Christ,' I said to Martha on the dashboard when I saw the gigantic image for the first time. 'I need to start learning my lines. Soon.'

105

And then I was sorry I'd said 'Holy Christ' in front of her. Because maybe she was a devout Catholic. Although that didn't tally with the fact that her bones were in a Church of Ireland graveyard.

106 'I saw myself on the back of a bus,' I said as I checked into a hotel in Kilkenny for my last reading before rehearsals.

'What bus?' the hotel receptionist asked.

'I was driving up from Waterford and at the ring road I came up behind an airport bus and it had my face on the back of it.'

She laughed.

'No, seriously,' I insisted, 'my face was on the back of the bus.'

She became almost hysterical.

'Honestly,' I said, pleading with her. 'I'm not mad.'

Her laughter abated and I could see the thought lodging in her brain. Madness. To change the subject I said, 'I need a massage. Urgently.'

She stopped laughing altogether.

'There's a spa at the other side of the motorway,' she said, a bit wary of me now, and I thanked her and finished the checking-in process.

That afternoon, I drove across town to the spa, where I was led into a dark room by a girl in a white coat called Susan.

'If you could just pop out of the trousers and shirt,' she said, 'and hop up on the table.'

As I turned around to glance at the table, Susan disappeared. A long massage table with a hole in one end dominated the room. There were candles on the floor and on a small desk, and soft music played in the background. I undressed as far as my underpants and stretched on the table, covering my pants with a towel. And I waited for Susan. When she reappeared, she applied her warm hands to the muscles of my thighs, rubbing warm oil deep into the skin, and worked her way up and down both limbs from thigh bone to ankle.

'You're very stressed,' Susan said.

'It's my mother,' I explained. 'I'm doing a book tour, and each night I go onstage and tell funny stories about her. They are all true. And I loved her. But we had a complex relationship and it makes me feel very lonely when I talk about her. And next week I'm starting rehearsals for a play in Dublin and I'm noticing my face on posters everywhere and it's making me very nervous.'

'And you write in the newspaper as well,' she said.

'Yes,' I replied, 'and that too is difficult because I say personal things about my feelings but afterwards I feel exposed and vulnerable.'

'I know,' she said, 'because I've read your columns.'

'Thank you,' I said, not knowing what was the right thing to say and feeling warm now as she worked up towards my spine, neck and arms and all across my back with her firm hands.

'Why do you talk so personally in the newspaper and onstage?'

'It's the only way I can break the isolation I feel.'

But that didn't answer the question. In truth, I don't know why I live my life so openly.

108 So after a while I said to her, 'Maybe I don't believe I exist. My depression gets really bad when I'm lying in bed, alone in the house, and I'm aware of the room and the bedclothes and I can see the room and the window and the trees outside but I'm not certain that I'm there. That frightens me.'

Susan didn't speak. Her fingers still worked on through the muscles of my neck.

'And only when I write about what has happened to me that I really believe it has any substance. It's the same with my feelings. It's only when I say, "I love you" that I know I love you. It's only when I say, "I am afraid" that I know I am afraid.'

'Your mother died,' she said.

'Yes.'

'And you never hugged her?' she continued. Clearly she had read my previous books.

'Correct.'

But I said no more. I had spoken too much. It was too confessional. And now I was embarrassed. Susan worked in silence after that, allowing her hands to sink deep into the muscle tissue of my body.

'God bless,' she said as I left, and the sweetness of it almost made me cry.

When I was back in my hotel room, I whispered to the crow on the tree outside the balcony of my bedroom. 'Do you think that I am a shallow person?'

The crow said nothing.

'Fuck it anyway, Mister Crow. Don't you start judging me.'

The crow turned his head, uttered a crow grunt and then a low, soft cackle.

I was still on the balcony of that hotel two days later when the sun was eclipsed by the moon. And just beyond the balcony was a tree where two crows were harvesting dead twigs in their fierce beaks. They would land, gather and then fly off with a mouthful of forestry. Apparently crows start building nests around St Patrick's Day. My mother used to light fires in all the rooms on Patrick's Day to ensure that no crow would select our chimney pots to start a new family.

I kept a close eye on the crows in Kilkenny. I had

golloped down my prunes and scrambled eggs in five short minutes at the breakfast table just to get back to the balcony and watch what might happen to them when the skies darkened. By nine o'clock, the morning resembled a day in December and the crows went mad.

I supposed they didn't know why it was getting dark; the poor creatures hadn't evolved far enough to conclude anything ontological about the nature of the universe. But their eyes bulged with fear and they began arguing with each other about the branches.

Then the sun returned, and I saw in their big black eyes a sense of relief, although there was still something ferocious about their huge grey beaks.

I could watch crows for hours.

And I liked being human, so when the eclipse was over and the sun returned, I went down into the lovely streets of Kilkenny, with no great purpose except to sit in a restaurant drinking coffee and watch other humans. In fact, after three shows in the Kilkenny region and three nights in the hotel, I decided to spend two further days resting on the balcony and staring at the crow-black feathers, grateful that I had been born a human and not a bird.

On Sunday morning, I checked out of the hotel before noon and headed for Dublin to begin rehearsals for *The Field*.

When we began to read the play, we came across a

scene about birds. A night scene in which two men sit in a field and talk about crows, wondering what do crows be thinking when they sit in a field.

'Can they talk to one another? I'd swear they have a lingo all of their own,' one character says in the play.

'Who's to say?' the other character replies. 'Who's to say?'

III

The Play

Touring around with a book and offering readings is one thing; theatre is something else entirely.

It's very different when there is a cast and a creative team involved and everyone has to follow precise rules of engagement with the audience. There's no space for chaos. There are disciplines to be followed. Lines to be learned. Things to be said in the same manner every night. It's a very different way of telling stories, although I love it because storytelling underpins all theatre, even at the highest level.

Europe was first imagined by peasants and refugees, penniless and poor. Fleeing wars and seeking refuge, they connected with other strangers, exchanged ideas and stories from a thousand villages until, through the centuries, they had forged a rich and diverse consciousness in literature, music and theatre. For me, Europe is not a set of national identities. It is a list of names: Lorca, Genet, Kafka, Beckett, Górecki and ten thousand more.

The stories that I weave onstage come from a rustic tradition, and my performance is a folk entertainment. My antics onstage are not far removed from the chattering grannies at the firesides of long ago, weaving stories of love and hate, of sex and death, for anyone who would listen.

But the possibility of Europe was born in such antics – in folklore, in stories around the fireside and, later, in cafe gossip.

Storytelling is a peasant craft, but it's also the backbone of high culture as it manifests in the sophisticated glitter of magnificent theatre halls or on the stages of Europe's greatest cities.

116

I went to London frequently to see actors like Mark Rylance in shows such as *Endgame*, Beckett's one-act play about a man who behaves badly and ends alone in a depopulated world or *Jerusalem*, a more recent masterpiece of English theatre about a waster who dispenses drugs and alcohol to the motley crew of young people who gather around him.

In *Endgame*, Mark Rylance was required to sit immobile in an armchair on castors for the entire play. In *Jerusalem*, his portrayal of Rooster Byron was so physically alive that I could never resist the possibility that he might transform into a rooster before my very eyes.

Mark Rylance is a great actor, and London is a place of high culture and I always love going there.

I remember looking out a hotel window in 2009 when I'd travelled over to see *Endgame*.

The sky was blue and I could hear the bells of St Paul's Cathedral, up the street, calling me to prayer

I lay on the bed, reciting poems by Wordsworth, and later I walked up into the cathedral, pushed in the heavy, creaking oak doors and found my old refuge.

What drew me in was the hope of incense and the certainty of a sanctuary lamp as red and delicate as the one from my childhood in Cavan. I'd grown up with that soft red flame as a sign of refuge, in clouds of incense as alluring as the aroma of apple tarts in a warm oven.

For me, the sanctuary lamp was the certain sign of an invisible and magical presence that intruded into the banal realism of childhood.

The lamp in Cavan Cathedral was cupped in an ornate silver bowl and hung like a pendulum from the high dome, flickering in midair above the altar. Whenever the oak doors were opened, a sudden wind would eddy down the aisle causing the lamp to shudder and the delicate flame in the red cup would flicker and I would feel the event reverberate in my heart like some act of nature that would silence Job.

Even the white wafer that floated above the head of the bleary-eyed priest at Mass, in a cloud of his own aftershave, was not merely a sign or symbol for me, but the very bread of angels.

The broken Jesus, stretched by the palms of his hands along the cross beam between the nails, thorn-headed and gory, was nonetheless a token of love, just as precious to me as my one-eyed teddy bear.

Wittgenstein said that religious behaviour was like kissing a photograph of the beloved; but in my Catholic childhood it was not an image that my lips touched but the real presence. It was the real presence that my tongue balanced inside my clenched teeth. That sacred presence which pervades all cosmic life, cleaving to the roof of my little mouth as I swallowed God in an act of single pointed devotion when I was seven years of age. Maybe it is the loss of it all that makes watching Beckett's plays so satisfying.

What brought me to *Endgame* was Tom Hickey, considered one of Ireland's greatest actors and a friend for many years. He was playing the part of Nagg, a legless character imprisoned in a dustbin whose head emerged at regular intervals to gnaw at a bone or offer a gesture of affection to his lady companion, who lived in the adjoining bin.

The text was beautiful. I felt devotion to the players. And I wanted to applaud every sentence.

I stood outside the stage door later, as rain lashed the roofs of the taxis. Up the street, outside Bistro Italiano, two waiters in black shirts and trousers were on a smoking break. They argued furiously with each other about who was the boss.

When Tom Hickey emerged from the stage door, he was laughing and distraught.

'What's the matter?' I asked.

He told me that as he was coming down from his dressing room to go onstage, he'd got into the lift as usual and pressed the button but nothing had happened. The lift door wouldn't open. It wouldn't move. He was trapped inside. He had been able to hear the voices of other actors onstage and knew his cue was coming in a matter of minutes but he hadn't been able to get free. He had banged and banged, his stress levels rising and then finally, at the very last moment, a carpenter had broken open the door and he was quickly binned and delivered to the stage, just in time for his first line.

The play had continued seamlessly, the audience none the wiser.

'But Jesus,' he declared, 'it was a close call.'

We dined on battered haddock in a restaurant up the street and joked about his ordeal.

'My God,' he exclaimed as he laid down the knife and fork on his plate, 'you're on your own when you're stuck in a lift! That's for sure!'

After dinner, he headed for the underground and I walked back up Fleet Street. The bells of the cathedral tolled for midnight. That was in 2014.

Two years later, at the end of April 2016, *The Field* opened at the Gaiety. I was playing the Bull McCabe. The playwright's widow, Mary Keane, came to the opening and she loved the show and my daughter took photographs of us both in the bar later in the night. In all the years I had attended theatre and admired actors, I had never dreamed of such a moment. Film-makers and television personalities, country people from Kerry and Donegal, flocked around me, speaking with enthusiasm about the performance. I was both exhausted and exhilarated. I should have been happy. In a way, I was. Except that it was the opening night. It was only the beginning. There was a month and a half to go, with shows every night of the week and twice on a Saturday.

The first scene opened with a tattered old tramp called Bird coming into the bar looking for a drink. It's morning time. The son of the publican is minding the shop. The Bird asks for a drink, as he is cold. He warms himself by the stove. He gets his drink. Soon the publican arrives and the son is dismissed, leaving the publican and the Bird to chat idly until the widow arrives.

The publican is also an auctioneer and the widow has come to sell her field. The Bird listens attentively. When she's gone, the Bird exclaims to the publican, 'The Bull McCabe won't like it.'

Up until that point, I'm in my dressing room, listening to the drama on the intercom. When the Bull is mentioned, I head out, crossing a corridor and into the backstage area, which is dark and where Fiona Bell, the actress playing the publican's wife, Maimie, is pacing in the corner, quietly rehearsing her lines, and the assistant stage manager, a young woman with fair skin, stands waiting for me. As I approach, she stands and asks me what I've got.

I take ten shilling coins and a wad of old Irish pound notes from a back pocket. I show her a watch that I have in my breast pocket. I show her my peaked cap. She allows me through. All these props are essential and every evening at the same time, she blocks my way until they are checked.

Then I go through another door that leads to a staircase taking me down to the basement, I go through more doors, following a tunnel underneath the stage and return up by a further stairs to the stage-right area. When there, I go through the door to backstage again.

The actor playing the policeman in the show is sitting alone on a stool, very still, as if meditating. Another assistant stage manager with headphones sits just behind the set and chews gum. I sit beside her and listen to the drama unfold onstage between the Bird and Maimie. They chat about her hard life, as a woman, and she bemoans the overbearing masculinity of a world in which her husband chastises her even if she goes to the hairdresser.

The Bird compliments her on her beauty, the finest woman in Carraigthomond, he declares, although he's just trying to cadge another drink. I wait for my cue.

At a certain line in the dialogue, I move closer to the

rear of the set. The actor playing my son arrives. He's young and looks rough, and we shake hands. This is our first moment onstage for the evening. Our hands clasp firmly. We say nothing. It's a sort of benediction, one to the other.

Suddenly, I hear a line.

'Spell "access"?' the publican's wife says.

'A–X–I–S,' the Bird intones.

And we burst into the world.

Into the imagined world of a bar in Kerry in 1965, and I lose myself and become the gruff, dark farmer by the name of Thaddeus McCabe, otherwise known as the Bull.

The audience, in the stalls, the circle, the grand circle and the gods, become even more attentive. It's not something to my credit, but they have been waiting for the Bull. In fact, their hushed attention frightens me because they have come from all over Ireland, many of them familiar with the play and many of them having been actors in various amateur drama productions up and down the country. And they have come to see the Bull.

I even sense that they love the Bull. His ferocity, his violence, his rage and insensitivity to women doesn't put them off. Because he is 'their bull, their wild man, their dark afflicted hero'. I hear a swoon every night. Not because of anything I've done, but because when they see the Bull in his ragged coat and cap, holding his stick aloft, they recognise him. They acknowledge him as an icon, risen out of their own dark unconscious. And my task for the evening has begun.

The Bull has heard that the widow wants to sell the field to the highest bidder. He is happy enough with that, although he has been renting the field from the widow for years, and it was the manure of his cattle that has made the field rich, and he has kept his cattle on it because it has a passage to water for his animals, and he doesn't have any other passage to water. But the publican says it will go to the highest bidder.

The Bull says he'll see to it that there'll be no other bidders. And so he concocts a plan with the publican.

The actor playing the garda sergeant who has been meditating in the wings since the curtain went up, now suddenly arrives in the pub.

He's enquiring about a donkey that was beaten to death and he suspects the Bull.

Of course the Bull is guilty, but the Bird provides an alibi for the night in question when the donkey was destroyed.

'We were at home playing cards,' the Bull says.

'Is that the truth, Bird?' the sergeant goes on to ask.

'Gospel!' the Bird replies, and the sergeant is defeated.

Off he goes, and the Bull remains, muttering to nobody in particular that such a sergeant might some night get his face kicked off, and all the guards in Ireland wouldn't find out who did it.

The lights go down.

The scene is over. I slip out the door in the dark, back through the wings, down the stairs, through the tunnel and on to the stage-left area, across the corridor that leads to the green room and back inside my own dressing room. I've been onstage for twenty minutes. I have about ten minutes' rest before the next scene.

By the time I reach my second entrance, the Bull McCabe has taken possession of me.

Then a new man arrives in the bar, home from London, boldly declaring an interest in the field. But he is verbally and viciously attacked by the Bull and warned not to bid at the auction. There is no ambiguity about this. The Bull has taken control of the bar as a community space. He has taken possession of the narrative. The story is now the Bull, the Bull, the Bull. And it is essential that the actor has by now taken possession of the stage.

He beats his stick against the bar, he breathes into the face of the frightened woman behind it and he informs all and sundry that when he and his son go out in the night to teach the stranger a lesson with their sticks, they must remain in the bar until the two rascals return. And when the guards come inquiring about what happened to the stranger, they will all swear that the Bull and his son never left the premises. Everyone agrees. Because nobody argues with the Bull.

Then the lights go down and the first half is over.

The audience is buzzing in the bar. They've enjoyed Act One. I lie on the couch in my dressing room and try to relax.

Fifteen short minutes later, I hear the stage manager's announcement: 'Beginners for Act Two onstage please.'

I leave the dressing room, with my cap and coat and the stick with which to kill the stranger.

I go out through the corridor, in the door that opens into backstage, dark and empty, since the other actors still linger in the green room finishing their tea and biscuits. I pick up a sandwich wrapped in paper that lies on a table of props and I put it in my pocket before going onto the stage.

The safety curtain is still down. There is a solitary tree in the playing area. It is surrounded by fog from a machine that has been working through the interval so the space feels desolate and cold and truly like a wild headland in the middle of the night.

Through the fog comes my son, a lean and loyal killer. We grip each other's hands again as we did at the beginning of Act One. There is a tight comradeship between us. We joke about how we will kill tonight. Maybe we will give him an extra wallop to the balls. Maybe a kick in the face.

The assistant stage manager with the fair skin hangs around us but does not interrupt. She has a microphone headset and she's listening to someone else.

After five minutes she gets clearance in her ears.

'OK, boys,' she says, 'that's clearance.'

And she leaves us alone under the tree in the middle of a field on the dark stage.

We wait. Tense. Nervous. My son sitting. Me standing above him, looking away from him.

Before us the safety curtain rises. I can hear the creak of the chains pulling it upwards into the space far above the stage. Up it goes, finally vanishing above our heads, exposing us and our field and our fears to the audience, some of whom are still straggling in the door with drinks in hand. And then the lights go up and a hush falls on the audience in the stalls and on the balconies and in the gods. All nine hundred of them are silent and, for a moment, I'm wondering what it is like to be out there, having paid money to see this play. To see this ritual of a killing. What is it like to have a drink at the interval and discuss the acting and then, with perhaps a second wine or a glass of lager, to return to the comfort of one's seat and wait in the dark to see the story unfold.

I don't know.

Because I am trapped in their imagination. I must

concentrate. And because the next one to break the silence will be me.

There is a faint sound of wind in the field where I stand with my son. The faint caw of a crow in the dark.

I offer him a sandwich. 'Eat that!' I say.

And he does and we wait again.

We talk about crows and how they might have a language of their own, and suddenly, unexpectedly, he asks me why I never talk to his mother and I tell him.

Many years ago, she allowed a tinker's widow put a pony in our fields. Fields that were then carrying fourteen cows when the grass was scarce.

'I was in bed when she told me,' I confess. And so I walloped her. I beat and battered her black and blue in the bed for her foolishness. And then I went out with a shotgun and killed the pony. A pony that had only one eye. But I shot him through the two. The good one and the bad one. A barrel at a time.

My son approves of the story. He admires his father. He sympathises with a man whose wife is the cause of all his sorrow.

'You had to do it, Da,' the son says.

Then he tells his father of the young woman he is courting. And how fine she would be at handling calves and pigs and how she has nine acres, and how she would make a good wife.

'I reared you well,' I say to him, admiring my own guts

and clarity in his eyes through the fog, because we are close now, very close.

In a few moments, the stranger will come through the fog and I will beat him in the stomach and on the face with the stick and my son will kick him in the head, as if he was kicking a football, until the wretched victim twitches and shivers and dies at my feet on the stage, and I will cry suddenly for my son to stop, and as my son vanishes across the fields, I will find myself alone.

I will cry out to God, to heaven, to the roof of the theatre, to the stalls and the three balconies, in horror and with remorse that I have done this deed, that I have crossed this threshold of killing. I will release from my gut a sense of shame and horror and expose it to the audience. A terrible stripping and flailing of my psyche will happen, induced by deep breaths from the pit of my stomach, as I have been practising in rehearsals for four weeks.

Then the killing is complete – until tomorrow night.

I leave the stage in darkness, following the assistant stage manager's little light that flashes in the wings to guide me off. I don't make eye contact with anyone as I follow the path through the light stands and the electrical wires around the wings until I find the door, then the corridor and open the door of my dressing room and close it behind me.

'I've done it again,' I whisper. 'He's dead. I've killed him again. I've killed a part of myself again.'

But it's the final scene that troubles me. The final scene is like a mountain I am never sure I can climb.

One night, I ate chocolate at the interval to give me energy, not knowing that chocolate can be lethal for the voice. I was only into the first speech of the scene when my voice began to fail and I could barely get to the end, croaking my way through speeches, barely audible.

After that I abandoned chocolate, but I took vitamin C energy tablets that the assistant stage manager bought for me each evening in a shop nearby. And I took Lucozade one night but that caused too dramatic a spike in energy. I went out into the first speech with great thrusting enthusiasm, feeling like Superman, the Bull McCabe brandishing his stick in the air above his head. But after ten minutes my energy collapsed, and I felt as if I was falling from a great height into an abyss. My legs went weak and I was powerless for the rest of the scene.

These mistakes would not occur with a seasoned actor but with me they occurred regularly during previews and frightened not just me but other members of the cast. My understudy for the role was an actor called Seamus O'Rourke, a monumental man who was playing the bishop and whose towering performance every night in the pulpit would bring a storm of applause from the audience. I would listen from my waiting position behind the stage set, admiring the thunder in his voice and the passion in his body and thinking to myself that there was the man who would be wonderful playing the Bull. But at least it was a consolation to know that if I tripped up badly in the part he would be there to take it on and the show would not collapse.

131

The thought that I might stumble somewhere along the line or that my nerves might break down or that I might be obliged to withdraw from performances terrified me. It was the possibility of shame and humiliation, and it hung over me and increased the anxiety that was keeping me awake at night.

How could I have got into this? I wondered. What kind of fucking idiot was I to presume I was capable of it?

I went to an actor in the company for support. Maria McDermottroe was playing the role of a dainty little lady with a strange sense of humour. She had two scenes, and all she did in them was laugh at her husband's jokes. But she took to the role with such imaginative power and energy that her laughter seared into the audience every night and made them laugh with her and pity her foolishness. It was a beautiful performance.

And she would come to my dressing room sometimes and give me words of encouragement or advice.

The cast were all star performers, gifted artists and tough professionals. At the beginning of the final scene, the Bird is interrogated by the sergeant and the priest. Mark O'Regan played the Bird with meticulous skill and beautifully controlled emotion. The cowardly Bird became incarnate. His creepy, sleazy answers revealed his terror. His refusal to disclose anything about the Bull. His fear of the Bull that prevented him from becoming a snitch.

And me, the Bull, sitting just off-stage, admiring the action on the stage manager's monitor: the finesse of control in the Bird's voice, the light and shade, the pacing, the timing of comic lines delivered with style each night, before the actor made his exit and passed by me as he headed for his dressing room. For him, the play was now finished for the evening. But not for me. For me, the last scene had just begun.

'How long more are you going to keep us stuck back there like prisoners of war?' the Bull wants to know as he bursts into this final scene. Because he and his son have been corralled in a room off-stage while the priest and the sergeant conduct interrogations with each individual one at a time.

But the Bull bursts out into the main area of the bar, impatient at waiting, and I begin to feel his anger and understand his rage because I too am long-suffering and my heart is a stone, but it's worth remembering that I was once a boy who brought flowers to his beloved.

I become livid from the moment I come into the bar and see the priest and the sergeant standing together, smug and intimate as if they had the world sewn up. Which they have.

And me? I have a son who is a monster. A child I'd love to fish with, but he has been schooled badly by me and kills humans not fish. And what we have done in the night troubles me.

Do I have problems? Real problems? I certainly have, and no money. And maybe I regret what I did all those years ago when I hit my wife in bed. Maybe it was a temper on me and I just didn't have the words to say sorry. Maybe I'm sorry I can't buy her a necklace like the one the publican's wife wears and which she fiddles with all the time unconsciously when she wants a ride.

I know these things because I'm instinctive. And I'm the person who controls the parish because I'm instinctive. I'm a cunning bastard. And I know how to elicit fear.

So who does the priest think he is? And the sergeant? Asking me which of us killed the stranger.

I tell him that maybe it was the tinkers. Or maybe it was

an ass or a pony gave him a kick. Or maybe he was down there in that field at midnight looking to fuck someone. Maybe some married someone. And who knows if the husband came along and a row broke out, and sure maybe some married man killed the stranger just to preserve the sanctity of marriage, Father. Wouldn't that be a good idea?

I got me boot in there all right.

But they keep coming at me.

The sergeant says, straight into my face, breathing on me, that it wasn't a donkey and it wasn't a tinker.

I says back that it wasn't Bull McCabe.

Because it wasn't. It was the son. And I'm so sick of them. They've been after me since the donkey was killed. And of course they have the law sewn up, all of them, and if it was one of them did something wrong, if it was the doctor that broke the law, or the schoolmaster or the sergeant, oh, there would be a way out, certainly.

But if it's me? If it's the ordinary poor man that loses his temper or kicks the guts out of some fucken donkey they're on the case right quick; they're down on me like a ton of fucken cement bricks.

So Father starts talking about goddy woddy.

'Do you ever think of God, any of you?' asks the sanctimonious bastard.

'He's the man I says my prayers to,' says I, 'and I argues with Him sometimes.'

And the priest says that God will be asking me some serious questions about this murder one day.

I tell him I'll be asking God some heavy-duty questions too, like why did He put so much suffering in the world, and how could he possibly make me one way and the priest another.

There's the question. There's where the drama ends for me. I nailed him. I made my case. So let them fuck off. The violence of the poor is simply a rage against those corrupt authorities that would judge us.

We are the unlettered ignorant poor of the earth. Is it wrong that I killed a stranger who was coming for my land? Coming to take it over and cover it with concrete and make a factory there, when I needed it because it was the only passage my cattle had to water, and if it was taken from me and I had no grass that would be an end to me and mine.

Is my tribe not allowed into the future? Do we have no part in the wider plans?

And you think I'm wrong to kill such a stranger! By the cross of Christ, I'd strangle him again, I'm thinking to myself, with my head fallen now on the bar and me leaning over and my cap in hand and tears coming down my cheeks.

But at least I got my say in front of that sanctimonious bastard.

And then the priest uses the widow.

What about the woman? he asks, after you killed her man.

One last sting from them as they leave. What will become of her?

And out they go the pair of them, the big tall sergeant with his stiff face and the buttery good-looking well-fed jowled cleric with his long black dress smelling of incense and coffin water.

And I can't resist. I let rip at the door as they leave.

I couldn't care less what will become of her, I tell the priest. No doubt she'll get another man without delay. She's pretty. And a dead man is no good to anyone. And the grass won't be green over his grave when he's forgotten. Yes, forgotten by all. By all except me.

There is the final blow.

'Forgot by all except me!'

That ends the play.

I'm shaking. I'm falling into a chair downstage centre. I stare into the middle distance. The emotions have been torn out of me. It's over. The lights go down. There is a short silence.

A hand claps. Another. And then hundreds of people are clapping and the lights come up and the cast returns, all smiles and relaxed, to stand in line as the audience now rise to their feet and we bow, and bow, and flee the stage. Flee the dark world of Carraigthomond for another night and I return to my dressing room.

Every night after the show, I walked home to Ranelagh, to a small apartment, picked up noodles or curry on the way and then, once inside the apartment, I turned on an electric fire, set up my computer and watched one more episode of *The Good Wife* as I lay back on the sofa eating my supper. It was as far away from the intensity of life on the stage as I could get. It was a cave, wherein I was enveloped by the soft shadows of Alicia Florrick as she moved across the screen, combing her hair or moistening her lips or hugging her children. And though I rarely followed the plot lines, her stillness and the grandeur of her femininity coupled with a bowl of noodles or chicken saag induced in me a sense of security and ease that made sleep possible.

On one particular Saturday night after a show, I went back to Leitrim in hope of a deeper refuge. But the house was empty, the roof was leaking and a huge stain was growing on the wall of the sitting room. There was mould growing behind the wardrobe in the child's room. The musty damp smell was everywhere.

Myself and the beloved had no more perfect emblem of love and devotion to each other than this cottage on the hill that had been our little paradise for twenty years. But it seemed that even the cottage was now crumbling. I couldn't bear another night in it, and the moment I woke the following morning, I headed back for Dublin.

At the roundabout just beyond Virginia there was a young woman standing on the roadside hitching, in a tartan skirt and a black plastic jacket.

I stopped.

She said she was coming from Donegal.

'I split up with my boyfriend,' she said.

'I'm sorry to hear that,' I replied.

'We had a caravan,' she said. 'At that big flat beach near the sand dunes.'

'Were you together for long?' I wondered.

'Since last summer,' she said, 'in the good weather. The caravan belonged to his uncle. Cement blocks holding it up. I got a flu in December from the damp mattress.'

'Where is he now?'

'I haven't a clue,' she said.

'So are ye what they call crusties?' I wondered, trying to be humorous. 139

She wasn't amused by the question, but her hair was purple.

'We're astronauts,' she said after a while. 'Most of the time we're in outer space,' and she chuckled at her own joke.

'What about you?' she asked. I could tell from her accent that beneath the dirty purple hair and tartan skirt and the stud in her lower lip there was oodles of self-confidence – like maybe she did honours maths at school or maybe her parents were always encouraging her to be a doctor before she decided to drop out.

'Did you ever consider going to a therapist?' I asked.

She laughed.

'Why would I do that?'

'I go to a therapist. Sometimes I suffer from anxiety,' I confessed. 'That's my problem.'

Her face opened, like she'd just woken up. It's amazing the power of a story, even if it's only two sentences.

'Go on,' she said, 'tell me more.'

'OK,' I said, 'I will.'

I paused and collected my thoughts and then spoke slowly, intimately, like there was no boundary between me and her.

'My therapist told me once that my mother's lack of physical intimacy with me could be the cause of my melancholy,' I said. 'She says that life without the tenderness of a mother can be traumatic and the wound can fester and cause problems in middle age when death becomes more real. So that's my entire story. I'm full of anxiety.'

'You're full of shit,' she said. For a moment, I thought she was serious. But then she laughed.

'No, but seriously,' she added, 'at least you're not boring.'

'Thank you.'

We were getting on like a house on fire as they say.

'And here's something else,' I added. 'My therapist tells me I need to give myself permission to be angry sometimes instead of always placating other people.'

'That's cool.'

'Yeah. It is. Like how can I avoid anxiety if I'm always trying to please someone else?'

'Too right,' she said. 'Although my boyfriend gave himself far too much permission to be angry,' she muttered under her breath.

Unfortunately, we were just hitting the M50 so a necessary silence developed that broke the flow of our intimacy, as I manoeuvred through lanes of traffic and negotiated a track towards the city centre.

'Do you ever go to the theatre?' I wondered.

'Jesus, no!' she exclaimed, horrified at the thought. 'That shite? Boring.'

There was nothing I could say after that. It was like I had a knife between my shoulder blades.

I dropped her off in the Phoenix Park, not far from the zoo. The last I saw of her was in the side mirror; she was hunched over a cigarette, trying to light it. 141

The old man in me was thinking that she should go and have a wash. The young man in me was regretting she hadn't recognised me from the posters.

After the final performance at the end of May, I went back to my dressing room, shaved the long beard I had grown for the role, showered and then packed my belongings into a rucksack. I walked down the corridor to the backstage door and into the night, a dark alleyway where homeless people drank from small bottles hidden in paper bags or the inside pockets of cheap anoraks. It was raining. Grafton Street was peppered with hens and stags in deep states of intoxication, stumbling around. I had already brought the car into town. It was stuffed with my belongings from the apartment in Ranelagh. I didn't want to spend another night in Dublin. I was heading for home. By the end of the run, I was exhausted and emptied and desperate to see my beloved again. Living out the emotional fracture of such a national icon as the Bull McCabe, a villain embedded deep in the collective unconscious, an icon of poisonous venom, and doing it seven times a week for a month and a half was not an easy task.

I left the city, knowing that the beloved would be on a flight the following day and that we would rendezvous in the hills above Lough Allen on the following Monday.

I parked up at the side of the cottage and took my bags inside. The rooms of the cottage were stuffy and musty, since nobody had lived there for months. I made a mug of tea in the kitchen and then went back outside to watch the light crossing the north. The sun falling beyond the slopes of the mountain in the west, but never quite fading. Slipping away but leaving a pale white glow, a milky wash on the horizon that shifted gradually across the north, so that the light never died.

At 4 a.m., it rose again, dawning majestically across the eastern mountains on the other side of the lake. Three months in the city, looking at my own dead face on billboards, going from one radio show to another and assuming the same disturbing role each night, putting on a peaked cap and walking the passage way underneath the stage and sitting with the meditating policeman and the assistant stage manager with her earphones and bursting into the limelight for two and a half hours to tell the story of a crazed farmer in Kerry had changed me. But I didn't realise it then.

All I knew was that I missed my beloved more than any other time in our life together. And that I loved our little cottage in the hills, our little paradise in the shelter of the woods. And that soon she would be with me again.

Midges in Paradise

There are lots of different expressions for the act of copulation. 'Bonking' reminds me of Laurel and Hardy. And 'shagging' has a softness that is useful at dinner tables. 'A ride' sounds a bit agricultural. 'A fuck' feels urban, and the phrase 'making love' is very old fashioned. And then there's the 'bang', the 'hump' and 'getting laid', which was in use a lot in my undergraduate days. A 'rogering' sounds very English, and there is a remarkable ferocity in the Gaelic phrase 'ag bualadh leathru' ('beating leather'), which sounds like a bit of an ordeal.

And I longed for her as I sat in the kitchen for hours staring at the presses above the worktop. All day I waited. But she didn't come on Monday evening. Her flight had been delayed.

On Tuesday morning, the sun crept over the rim of the mountain above the lake before I woke. I slid the patio door open and went outside. The yellow rose plants each in their separate pots had been battered by the winter wind. And their leaves still showed signs of blackspot.

The garden was overgrown because we had both been away. The lawn had turned into a rough field. The trees were ragged and dense. There was hogweed raising its head in the meadow. And creeping buttercup everywhere, tangled so densely through the long grass that when drizzle fell a yellow hue hung over the field. Whenever the drizzle stopped, the clouds turned purple and overhung the earth like the underbelly of a gigantic fish touching the tip of Sliabh an Iarainn and bringing an astonishing intensity to the yellow of the buttercup.

And the foxgloves were rising. Tall steeples that would soon be dressed in purple fluted petals along the ditches. I stepped down off the patio and walked through the long grass to the cliff's edge. Below me was the shale quarry that Sean Quinn had dug out fifteen years earlier and which closed during the recession. Beyond that was the lake, the entire length of Lough Allen, and in the distance the slopes of Sliabh an Iarainn.

I walked from the big meadow to the paddock, a narrow length of ground surrounded by a wooden fence. An enclosure stretching from my studio to the edge of the cliff above the lake. It too was wild with rushes and weeds, scutch grass and bindweed, dock leaves and thistles reaching to the heavens. Again, I walked deep into it and pulled away the long grass with my bare hands to find the slab of stone that covered the remains of a cat, Ronnie, who had been born in the drawer of a posh house in Greystones in 2007 but who had died of cancer three years later.

I went to visit each tree in the copse on the southern half of the property. The alders, oaks, chestnuts, willows and beeches. All of them high now, with huggable trunks as strong as pillars in the shaded interior. And I touched each one.

I strode into the centre of the wood where a single silver birch stood out. I placed my arms around her and hugged her tightly. I could feel the sway of her huge branches slipping into my body as if the tree was responding to my touch.

'I am home,' I whispered, as I held her tightly.

150 I woke at 9 a.m. on Tuesday, but still there was no sign of the beloved. I wasn't bothered. In fact, I had decided to begin work on the long grass immediately – the cat's tail and the Yorkshire fog, beautiful in their dance as the wind moved across the field. I got the lawnmower from the green steel shed and filled it with petrol. It jumped into life the moment I pulled the cord. The clouds dissolved; the sun came out and warmed the grass so that the midges were up almost immediately, alarmed at my attack on their perfectly incubated sleeping world. I had to lean the machine at an angle of 30 degrees in order to cut into the top of the wild grass, and then pull backwards, in reverse, at a lower angle to make any impact on the wilderness. I stopped for a mug of tea at eleven and, at lunchtime, I drove down to Drumshanbo and had a bowl of stew in the café section of the Gala shop. I bought a loaf of homemade brown bread, butter and a jar of marmalade and refilled

the red plastic petrol canister for the lawnmower at the filling station.

When I returned to the house, I expected to see her car parked beside my own. Expected to find her in the kitchen with her cases perhaps. But there was no sign.

I lay on the bed for the afternoon and in the evening turned on the TV, opened a bottle of wine and emptied it before I went to bed.

The next day, I woke at 6 a.m. and walked about the house. But still the silence was unbroken.

I brushed my teeth and had a piss and wiped the toilet seat with tissue paper. I went outside and then, suddenly, as I came around the gable end, I saw her car.

'Well, well,' I whispered, trembling.

Although, I continued walking all around the outside of the house in my slippers and dressing gown so that, when I found her, I was calm. She was on the patio in a white straw hat. She looked me in the eye and said nothing.

'Ah, you're home,' I said quietly, gently, as if she had just come back from a neighbour's house or as if she had just slipped out of the room for five minutes and not actually been away for months.

I wanted to hug her but I didn't. I couldn't.

I wanted to say, I have missed you, but I didn't.

It's as if the Bull McCabe was still a hard shell from which I couldn't release myself, a smell that lingered on my clothes, enveloped me in some kind of isolation.

I wanted to entice her into the bedroom while the sun was shining through the white curtains and the morning breeze was moving them. We would bathe afterwards and the entire day would still lie before us. But I didn't.

She smiled. 'Are you OK?' she asked.

'Yes,' I said, 'I'm fine.'

'I didn't want to wake you,' she said. 'I've been here for an hour.'

'I was exhausted,' I said. 'I heard nothing.'

'I see you've been busy,' she said, pointing at the little infraction I had made into the long grass. I didn't say anything in reply.

'So is it over?' I wondered with far too much haste. After all she was hardly in the door. 'Is your work in Warsaw finished?'

'Wait until I make tea,' she said, smiling. 'Then I'll tell you all about it.'

Suddenly she jumped up in terror.

'Midges,' she cried. 'At this hour of the morning.'

I stood staring at her. I didn't move.

'Come inside,' she pleaded, as she fled to the sun room, 'they're getting at me.'

She went into the sun room but I stayed another few minutes at the wrought-iron table, allowing them eat my ears as I sipped a glass of orange juice she had left behind and watched them crawl through the hairs on the back of my arm. Crawling too on the soft flesh under my arm, above the wrist where there was no hair. And feeling them bite. Feeling for a moment, the exquisite sensation of being someone else's dinner. And then I went inside, sliding the patio door behind me.

'You've brought them in,' she said, because the midges were dancing around my head. She had her back to me as she wiped the sink with a cloth. Clearly she wasn't answering my question.

'I think I'll do a little more work on the garden this morning,' I said.

'Be careful of them,' she said. 'You'll be eaten alive.'   153

I didn't lose control immediately in the garden, but eventually I attacked the long grass with a strange rage, strimming with the insanity of a pilot carpet-bombing Dresden, as if somehow this demonic act of aggression on the midges might quieten them. It didn't.

'So she's not finished in Warsaw,' I muttered. 'Clearly there's a pattern emerging, is there not?'

The midges came towards me in such thick clouds that I could barely see anything. I was wearing a hundred-percent-polyester screen over my face and something that resembled a jungle combat hat, which I'd bought in the pound shop, so that I could easily have been mistaken for a soldier facing enemy fire, screaming, 'Fuck yis! Yis bastards! Yis little fucken cunts!'

But maybe there was no point in strimming any more weeds. Not if she wasn't going to be around. Not if she was going back to Warsaw. It was only mid-morning but I could hear the sound of domestic appliances in the house. I abandoned the garden and went up to the patio, sat on a chair and listened to the washing machine and the dishwasher rumbling away like jazz singers trying to find a new coherence.

In fact I was wrong. I thought she was avoiding the question. But she was only waiting for the right moment to speak.

A few weeks later, when the light of heaven itself seemed to be falling on Ballinaglera across the water of the lake, she explained it all then. What a magnificent a journey she had been on, and how immeasurable was the allure of the icon, and how she would need more time.

'How much more time?'

'I could go in September, and be back next June,' she replied.

Nine months more before she finished the project. And my immediate concerns were about me. I'd be alone. Sitting by the fire again – not just for part of the winter but all winter.

'I'll be home in June,' she promised.

'Sure that's not a long time at all,' I said. And privately I was wondering where all this would end.

I suppose there is something helpless about an ageing male. It's as if he is destined for solitude as he approaches death. On the threshold of old age, when a man sees himself withering for the first time, he panics. He needs his partner's hand in ways he never did before. He says 'hold me' too often, until it sounds selfish.

He walks alone and broods – like I did, up the hills as far as Scardan waterfall in the evening light. The waterfall in full flow after heavy rain in the flooded streams.

The waterfall was gushing, bloated and loud and it fell over the cliff in a rage, as I leaned across the stone bridge to hear it and then headed off up the looping narrow mountain path known as the horseshoe, taking me upwards for a short while towards the curlews, the small hawks and the windmills, and then around in a circle, past boggy headlands of bilberry with the lake in view, as the road returned to the waterfall after about fifty minutes. A solitary man on his evening walk.

And I got addicted to the remote for the television again, which was a bad sign. It was as if I couldn't live without something in my hand, some sense of control, some assurance that the universe would not overpower me. When we were together we sat shoulder to shoulder on the sofa, and the remote control was like a wand that shielded me from intimacy. And when I went walking I took my phone with me. It never rang, but I looked at it every few minutes, just in case.

Although there were times when she came too, during that summer. And she liked to find wild rasberries or touch the tiny white, yellow and purple flowers that grew on the ditches in July. And even in company, I felt I was taking on the crooked style of a man who cannot name his fears. A man who cannot quite tell his story honestly. A man in his sixties who is beginning to experience for the first time the invisibility of the elderly.

And so we walked. Uneasy. I suppose like many couples with grey hair and creaking bones and malfunctioning organs. We walked in silence because we had too much to say without knowing how.

I still had enough of the Bull McCabe inside me to hide tender emotions. And yet I could be possessed with rage and fury when I walked alone into the garden.

I flung myself at the weeds and the field mice as if I despised them.

I attacked plants with slash hooks and clippers and various blades. I grunted at them with rude and unconscious hostility. The mower sliced who knows what into little pieces and, strangely, that pleased me.

'Come here, you bastards,' I'd say to the soft branches of the beech hedge as I clipped them or the nettles under the oak trees.

And when the work was done, I would walk away from the garden on a Saturday afternoon like a warrior, dehydrated and emotionally exhausted, like a boxer after a good bare-knuckle fight.

She would look at me through the kitchen window but she never asked why.

And whenever an unexpected bill arrived in the post, or an invitation came to a distant relation's wedding, or cat poo suddenly manifested on the bedroom carpet, I would focus on the garden and go there, and remain under the trees even if it was raining, and vent my rage on whatever was in sight. And I carried the slash hook with me wherever I wandered.

The sheep didn't know how lucky they were. Three of them just wandered into the garden one day. At first, I thought it was funny so I took a photograph: a mammy sheep and two big girl sheep sitting in a single huddle beside the beech hedge. Then I sent the picture to the General.

'The new lawnmowers have arrived,' I texted, because he has one of those automatic machines that crawls around the grass all summer long keeping it manicured.

But the sheep decided to stay overnight at the door of my studio, and in the morning their droppings were everywhere.

Droppings is a nice word for it – but only the two big girl sheep left droppings. The mammy sheep left huge mountains of black stuff like miniature slag heaps of coal and you couldn't call it anything but shite. It was lucky for the sheep that I value shite. So I shovelled it in a bucket and tossed it into the rose pots.

I could have gone into the house shouting, 'Damn those sheep, I have shite all over my shoes.' Or worse still, 'I'm after walking that shite onto the carpet.'

But I didn't. I stepped gingerly and held my breath and looked into their lovely big sheep eyes and said, 'OK, OK, this just means more dung for the roses.' But it was a close call. The knuckles of my hand were white as I gripped the slash hook and flailed the air above their heads to get them out of the garden.

If it was too wet for the strimmer or the lawnmower, I would flail nettles with the slash hook.

And when it was too wet for even a slash hook, I would sit listening to corncrakes on YouTube.

Little hens that used to come up from South Africa to lay their eggs in Donegal, nesting in the dry meadows that I could smell through the wide open windows of my father's A40, as we drove to Bundoran on our holidays in 1966.

'But where are they now?' I asked myself. 'Where are they now?'

I love the rugged landscape of the Donegal coast so much that it gave me an idea. One morning as I was looking at the beloved across the table of toast and boiled eggs, I made my move.

Of course, I should have just told her the whole story. That I was becoming invisible and it frightened me. That I had taken on a role onstage that I wasn't able for. And now I was spiralling down into a well of anxiety that was paralysing, even when the remote for the television had slipped into the crevices of the sofa and I couldn't find it. I was gripping the steering wheel of the car too tightly.

I took a chainsaw to the branches of a few trees one day and was slicing them into little logs for the fire when I had a sudden flash of rage about Japanese bindweed. Suddenly, the saw slipped and tore into the leg of my trousers. It didn't break bone or even flesh but it was close. The trousers were in flitters and my hands were shaking as I changed into another pair. But I decided not to tell her. I suppose there's nothing as devious as a man who has lost the thread of his own story. A man who is no longer sure who he is. And there's certainly not much chance of a laugh, nevermind intimacy, with such a beast.

And yet despite all that, in the teeth of all that, I decided a holiday might be the solution. We should go away for a few days, I thought. There was absolutely nothing wrong with me that a few days in Donegal wouldn't fix.

So in a fit of passion, to make us both new again, to begin again and become one, I said, 'Listen. Why don't we go away?'

'But I've just come back,' she said.

'No, I mean somewhere close – like Donegal. Right now. For a holiday. What do you say?'

We packed the car. I brought walking boots and rain clothes, leggings, plastic containers for walking, a backpack and a walking stick. She brought her iPad.

For a while, we enjoyed a great warmth from each other. A cosiness in the Mitsubishi ASX cocooned us as we drove through the glens of Leitrim.

We drove up through Manorhamilton at two in the afternoon, without any certainty about where exactly we might end up, apart from the fact that we intended heading west along the Donegal coast road.

We parked on the street in Killybegs outside the Bay View Hotel and asked Holly at reception if she had a room. She did. A lovely big white room with a table to work at and a view of the harbour.

Later, we dined at Castle Murray House Hotel and Restaurant. I had steak as a main course and for starters I chose monkfish baked in butter with mozzarella cheese. The dining room was calm. There was no disturbing music. Just an air of posh awe hanging over the other tables as diners spoke and ate with a kind of quiet reverence and gazed at the sea and mountain beyond the window where the evening sun was slanting its light across the silver ocean.

161

'Andrei was asking for you,' she said. 'He'd love to meet you again.'

Andrei was a master icon maker she had been working with. I had met him once when we were first in Warsaw, a whiskey drinker, lean and intense, who spoke English with a nervous disposition. He always seeemed a bit shell-shocked. As if the police had just beaten him up and he was afraid to tell. He carried fear around with him like a headache, and he always kept an eye on the exits in any room, even when we were drunk.

When she mentioned him, I felt it was a way of signalling that she was firm in her resolve to return to Warsaw.

The next day we drove to Sliabh Liag and parked near the foot of the mountain. The viewing area wasn't crowded. Mostly Germans strolled around taking pictures of cliffs and ocean waves, of small hawks and tiny birds. A man was selling ice-cream and coffee from a van. We bought tubs of vanilla and two coffees.

We drove to St John's Point near Dunkineely, heading for the lighthouse. It is one of the longest peninsulas in the country, a paradise of isolation, with sea on both sides and haunted by beautiful townland names – the Turf Port, the Lobster Rock, the Brown Hill, the Pissin Hole, Geordie, the High Nose, the Winnie Mills, Tail of Acre and the Giant Stones.

We stopped at a weaver's shop. The weaver was a young woman who was delighted with customers and she gave us a demonstration of the loom at work. I could have sat watching her weave for hours. The clank and swing and clop of it reminded me of horses pulling drays of textile on cobbled streets in ancient days.

'I have to be utterly focused,' she said. 'I even forget to eat sometimes. But it balances well with horses. When I've been too long at the loom, I can muck out or ride down along the beaches. The horses and the weaving sit well beside each other.'

As we drove farther towards the lighthouse, my beloved said, 'That weaver is like an icon maker. The same energy. The same result.'

We sat in the bracing wind underneath the lighthouse 163 wall for a long time without speaking.

The wind would not allow us.

As they say, 'If you want to go farther than the lighthouse you have to take a boat.'

'I will miss this when I'm back in Warsaw,' she said.

I looked at her and saw a stranger. Anxiety had clouded me. Made me forget that only in the entanglement with others can I be human. It's a kind of madness: a self-obsession, a belief more troublesome than faith in God. This was the belief that there are no gods and that I could stand alone.

She had a lunch packed and she opened the plastic box and took out slices of avocado.

'I love avocados,' she said, and I thought, Does she indeed love avocados? All this time, without me even noticing?

And I wondered, What is it like to be her? To be in

love with fruit. Because I had seen her one day in the garden and heard her grunting in the forest of artichokes, her spade hitting the stones of the dainty border, and I wondered even then, who is that person in the artichokes? Could I have been with her for so long without knowing anything?

'I will miss all this,' she said.

I tried to imagine myself in winter, writing a book, alone, and her in Warsaw.

'We could stay here,' I suggested, 'and use the lighthouse as a studio.'

'You could always come to Warsaw,' she replied.

Me? I thought. Go to Warsaw? Is she mad? To be trailing behind her like an old dog?

Not me, I thought. No way.

'Sure I'll be fine at home on my own,' I said, burning with shame that I felt like a boy inside, madly in love but with no words to articulate it. Until she came closer and touched my arm and, for a moment, I was released from the burden of being me.

And when we came back from Donegal there were four magpies on the lawn. And that night we slept in separate beds, because sometimes a partner's snoring can waken the other, and sometimes going to the bathroom wakens the other, and people often find it hard to fall back asleep when they have been woken. We used to lie side by side for hours, each absorbed in private anxieties, until eventually I would say, 'Are you awake?' and she would say, 'Yes,' as if admitting to something terrible.

People over fifty just don't sleep that well. They wake suddenly, as if staring into an abyss.

It might be money. A bill not paid. Or a birthday forgotten. It might be a stomach pain or a strange lesion on the skin or an irritable bowel. Some casual and innocent thing that to a person at the end of middle age can signify trouble ahead.

So, occasionally, we sleep in separate beds, but close enough to hear each other, close enough to meet cheerfully in the kitchen at four in the morning over a boiling kettle or beside the fridge, with the knowledge that sleep comes now with toast and marmalade as sure as it used to come in the wake of fierce love.

It was half five in the morning when she came to me, and we lay there listening to the birds. I wanted to make love, but my body was sluggish, so we lay waiting for the universe to surprise us.

Eventually she said, 'Let's go for a walk.'

It was 6 a.m. The sun was already matured in the sky as we walked to the gates, the black wrought-iron gates that had come from a convent in Castlerea. We paid fifty punts for them in 1993. We were leaning over them, looking down the road, down the hill where we could see Carrick-on-Shannon in the distance, fourteen miles away, and Sheemore to the south.

We had not spoken since we'd left Donegal.

'I'm tired,' I said.

'That's OK,' she said.

And she kissed my cheek.

'You look well after the play in the Gaiety,' she said.

'You look well after your three months in Warsaw,' I replied.

We wanted to hear the birds then so we both kept quiet.

'Look there,' she whispered.

There was a magpie sitting on a branch of the alder tree beside us. Then another appeared. Then they both vanished.

A farmer was driving a tractor past our gate one day in June, heading towards fields farther up the mountain. He looked sideways and saw me running and screaming up the lawn. The distraction almost caused him to crash the tractor into the ditch. Then he stopped, hopped off the tractor and came in the gate to see if I was all right. By then, I was on the patio and she was spraying my arse with a concoction of citric juice and washing-up liquid which she swore by for cleaning greenfly from the roses.

'But they're not greenfly,' I told her. 'They're midges.'

'Right enough,' the farmer agreed, 'that's what they are.' He had come softly onto the patio, his huge red hands rolling a little cigarette and his blue eyes glistening beneath a straw hat.

'Oh, they're a fucken curse,' the farmer said.

'Bastards,' I said.

'A terror,' the farmer said.

'If it wasn't for the midges,' I said, 'Arigna would be paradise.'

'Paradise,' the farmer repeated.

We all sat on the black wrought-iron garden seats and stared at the garden, like we were looking across the battlefield at enemy lines.

The creeping buttercup. The long grass. The Yorkshire fog billowing in the breeze. The foxglove steeples swaying from side to side. The floating leaves of the beech trees and alder in the afternoon breeze. The dog roses. The Albertine roses. The pink wild rose that my father had brought from Clare to Cavan sixty years ago.

'Yis have the place shining,' the farmer said.

I didn't speak. But I was savouring the praise in silence.

She made tea. She rubbed more washing-up liquid on my face and arms and the farmer laughed.

'They're all over his body,' she said.

The farmer was staring at the lawn and the shrubs.

'It would remind you of Vietnam,' he said.

We drank the tea in silence.

'So you like it here,' the farmer said, because one thing leads to another and he hadn't come into the garden just to rescue me from wild midges. Nor was he on his way up the hills to mow fields.

'Yes, I do like it here,' I admitted.

'I was talking to Mr Cafferty the other day,' the farmer

said. 'He was telling me you're thinking of cutting a few trees.'

There were four withered Scots pines to the north of the house that could have been taken out to make the others look better. 'It would tidy up that area,' I said, 'if we took out the ones that are not thriving. The rest would stand out more elegantly against the northern sky.'

And I invited the farmer to come walk around the house so I could show him.

'It wouldn't be worth your while tossing those trees,' the farmer said. 'There isn't enough timber there to do a single winter. And with all those phone wires and electricity cables criss-crossing them it wouldn't be worth the bother.'

'But I want them for firewood,' I explained.

'I could bring you a load of hard wood,' the farmer suggested.

'I have no woodshed. I'm hoping to get someone to build me one later in the summer.'

The farmer said, 'I could toss you in a load and you could leave them out on the grass to season, and then put them in the shed when you have it built.'

That seemed like the wrong way around.

I said, 'I don't want to be shifting blocks twice. Bring them in September. I don't have time for doing it now. I'm under pressure at the moment. My beloved is just back from Warsaw. She was away for four months. And now she is thinking of going back for another year. So we have a lot to do.'

The farmer said, 'You're working hard, but remember you can't take it with you.'

'I know,' I replied. 'I know. As they say, there's no hitch on a hearse.'

'Ah well, in fact there is,' he said. 'Cos I seen one only last week in Longford. And they had this little trailer behind with all the flowers in it. Wasn't that a clever idea? Whatever bastard thought that up?'

'Bring the blocks in September,' I suggested again.

'Fair enough,' the farmer replied. 'I'll do that.' And he stared at the pair of us, the happy couple, from under his battered straw hat, his blue eyes like the ocean and his wrinkled face as dark as leather.

'You're no joke,' he said. 'The pair of ye.'

'What do you mean?' I wondered.

'You're the writer,' he said, as if it was an accusation.

'Yes,' I admitted, 'I'm the writer.'

'My father was in the American army,' he said. 'He used to be always talking about the Viet Cong. But he had books as well. Books about monks. They were no joke either. The monks in Vietnam.'

He grinned and mounted his tractor and flung the butt of his cigarette into the wind and drove out the gate, still muttering something and chuckling to himself.

I turned my face to the long grass again. I had about

one-third of the strimming done. The day had settled. The sun rose very high and burned the garden and dried the grass and pierced the shadows beneath each tree. The grass was warm and wet and steamy. Something stirred in the undergrowth. Midges again, perhaps, but then I saw it was the pigeon. The pigeon stuck its head up and looked at me. Behind him, the swallows were flying low. Not just low. They were skimming the grass where I had just strimmed. They went back and forth along the treeline, dipping suddenly, swerving, turning. I guessed it was the new clutch. The newborns out of nest and playing with each other, just as we used to, me and her, when we were young and had abandoned the city and come to the hills above Lough Allen like refugees from a broken world. When we fell in love with Leitrim.

171

Of course, Leitrim has changed so much in recent years that nothing is predictable anymore. In the old days, there was just one Leitrim: an emotionally impoverished world. A grim island of silence and obedience, well described by John McGahern, of dark fathers with gorilla paws that could clasp a spade like a toothpick and open a ridge of soil in virgin ground with the delicacy of a surgeon slicing his way into living flesh. A world of little shops where the doorbells were cheerless and tinkled with the temerity of a keening woman's cough and where there was always an elderly lady behind the counter slicing ham in silence.

But there are other Leitrims now. There are sculptors

from America and England and ceramic artists from Hungary. The pubs and hotels are alive with hen and stag parties, and the Glens Centre buzzes with radical political theatre and musicians that come from all over the world to gig.

And scattered along the slopes of various hills there are refugees from the urban jungles of Europe and English boys in cottages and mobile homes. They worry about fracking and have lonely hearts, like gardens choked with weed and as yet untended by psychotherapists.

172   There is another Leitrim too, hidden away between the hills, a kind of Germanic order, a neat organic world sectioned off by high-grade fencing wire, where people in greenhouses the size of little bungalows nurture gigantic cabbages and exotic fruits so juicy that John McGahern's father might have self-combusted if he had ever tasted one.

And there is a Celtic Tiger Leitrim on the fringes of the big towns, where people still cling by their fingernails to the interiors of their grand houses, an affluent middle-class land of trim hedges where smooth-shaven office workers tend their lawns and their jawbones with equal attention, shaving in the gym on weeknights and clipping the grass down to its roots on dry Saturdays, while inside enormous kitchens and utility rooms the washing machines, dryers and dishwashers hum like a hive of bees.

When I was young I often sneered at men who took refuge in gardens. Politicians who retired were always doing it. Big fat English MPs with hairy eyebrows and turkey necks would tell the interviewer that they were looking forward to the garden, and the interviewer would say, 'What will you do?'

'I have a passion for hydrangea,' he might say or something similar. And I would laugh at the television. Such nerds, I thought, those politicians.

I sneered. Just as I sneered at older men with ponytails.

Until I found myself in the shimmering leaves of the beech trees seeking shelter and wondering was it possible that I had arrived at that moment of wisdom when a man lifts his hands from the plough, turns his back on the world and finds peace in the garden.

Was I finding my true nature as an emotionally detached zen monk?

Not a fucking chance of it. Yes, I was in love with the wilderness – and I got a sensual pleasure in sheltering beneath the trees – but I was as close to enlightenment as a cackling magpie.

In reality, the garden was just a space that separated me from her. A place where I could brood or rage or dream as I pleased. Whenever she did appear on the patio in a white straw hat, rubber gardening gloves and wellingtons, I fled somewhere else.

'Where are you going?' she'd ask.

'Petrol. I need to refill the strimmer,' I'd snap.

I remember one afternoon filling a canister with petrol at a filling station in Drumshanbo and then for no particular reason I abandoned the lawn and drove to Ballinamore.

Maybe because I needed to get my bearings once in a while during that summer. I needed to find again the soul of Leitrim, or reconnect with the wonders that we had found when we'd first come to this quiet corner of Ireland. I drove beyond Ballinamore and took a turn to the left, up a small lane, and parked beside the quiet and serene field where John McGahern had spent his childhood in the shelter of his mother. It's just a field now. The house seems to have dissolved, stone by stone into the air, and only the gateposts remain, with the rusting gate still hanging between them. On the ditches around the sloping field, there were alders and hawthorn. The field itself was full of yellow flowers. I leaned on the gate and clung to the serenity of it all for a moment and, for that moment, the sun came out and Leitrim appeared almost unbearably beautiful. Although it didn't cheer me. In fact, I almost suffocated with melancholy in that moment.

The farmer returned with a trailer of wood for the winter. He was probably my own age, but I knew nothing personal about him. Did he fear old age like me? Did he feel invisible on his tractor, driving along the road as fast, flashy cars passed him by? I don't know. But I suppose we're all human and so even standing beside a stranger can be an intimate experience.

As we were looking up at the trees, I noticed two old magpies sitting on the long, horizontal arm of the Scots pine. The arm moved in the wind and the magpies were unbalanced so they flapped up into the air and circled the house and then landed on the spruce tree at the north end of the property.

'I hate those bastards,' the farmer said.

I thought the farmer meant the magpies. But he was talking about the spruce trees. And he suggested we cut them down.

'They're dangerous,' the farmer said. 'Too close to the

house. They might come through the roof some winter's night.'

There was no point in trying to tell the farmer that I couldn't cut the big spruce because the old magpies had been lodged up there for years.

'You told me you would bring me hardwood logs in September,' I said, changing the subject.

'Ah,' the farmer said, 'there's no point in taking out the little ones. Them old dead things that is tangled in the wires. But that big fella. He's huge. You could get a winter out of him.'

I stared up at the majestic fifty-foot-tall spruce that has lived in the corner beside the gates for fifty years.

'Jesus,' the farmer said, 'I hate those bastards.'

The Builders

It's not that there was anything fundamentally wrong with the house. But there's always little things that you can find if you poke around with a negative attitude. And maybe I was trying to find something to keep the beloved at home. To entice her to stay.

So the kitchen was too cold. We could change that. The cupboards were cheap. We could get new stuff. The black cooker wasn't working – the door of the oven never closed properly. No problem. Replace it.

These were things I could have fixed. But they hardly warranted an extension.

I walked into the little bedroom where we had slept for a quarter of a century. It was hardly big enough to contain the bed. It definitely needed a transformation. But how?

There was an office on the far side of the wall with a separate entrance, so maybe we could cut through the wall and make one large bedroom.

There was no utility room off the kitchen, apart from a tiny scullery which was always overloaded with coats and boots and shoes and cat food. And there wasn't even a water supply in the house, apart from rainwater harvested from the roof. It ran down gutters and gullies into a cement water tank at the rear of the house, and from there, by way of a small motor, it was pumped up into the tank in the attic. It had suited us perfectly for twenty-three years but, all of a sudden, I felt it wasn't up to the mark.

Only the sun room was acceptable, an extension with an enormous window looking out on the trees in the garden. But, on the other hand, the gas in the double glazing had leaked out over the years and the window was so fogged up that it was hard to see anything through it. And there were no plug points. Plug points were not important in 1996, but with the addition of smartphone chargers, Sky TV, the Apple TV box and the DVD player, a room without plugs was a nightmare. If a woman had enough plug points, she wouldn't need to go to Warsaw. That was obvious.

If I could remake the house I might remake the entire universe. The mould that was growing behind the shelves in my old office was more than a stain on the wall: it embodied the relentless passing of time that was eating away at me.

The builder arrived for a chat on the patio. He brought his father with him, an elderly man who had worked on the house in the nineties, when his son was the barrow boy. Now the boy was the man, a contractor in his own right, and the father had come to see again the house that he had worked on. It felt like poetry. Me and the beloved would be young again in our little paradiso on the hills.

We drank tea and the old man told jokes, and myself and the builder walked from room to room.

'I just want to see what is possible,' I said, hoping that I had money to do whatever I wanted.

He said that remaking the kitchen and building a utility room might prove very expensive, and we were better to leave the toilet as it was.

I felt he didn't want to do anything.

'What about a new bedroom?' I wondered.

'But do you need a new bedroom?' he asked.

Having nothing else to chalk up as progress, I said, 'Yes, that's the main thing. We need to cut a hole in the bedroom, connecting it to the office, which I don't need anymore, and put on a further room at the far end of the office. Then we will have two big twin bedrooms, one for her and one for me, with lots of glass looking out on a patio. Because we need a new patio as well. We definitely need a new patio. That would make all the difference.'

'Right,' he said, 'so you want a patio?'

'Yes.'

'And an extra room?'

'Correct.'

'And have you drawn up a plan?'

'No.'

'Well, it's a lot to build from a plan in your head.'

'It's simple,' I said, slightly irritated. 'Just open the wall and make a big room. Then put a door in the far end and stick on another room. What could be easier?'

He looked at me. Opened his mouth to speak, but then said nothing.

'I'll have to put down a few figures,' he said eventually, 'and I'll get back to you but I suppose it could be done.'

The beloved had spent all the time listening to the old man telling jokes. She didn't show much enthusiasm for the plans, but I didn't think that was significant. Even the builder didn't show much enthusiasm for a while. Two months passed before he returned. On one occasion, he phoned me to check that we still wanted to go ahead. 'Are you definite?' 'Yes, I am.' And so he said he'd start in August.

It was 6 August when they arrived, at nine in the morning, two of them in a white Ford pick-up, three more in a white but rusting Berlingo van and a further two in the front cabin of a silver Mitsubishi jeep. They all smoked and made jokes with me about the rain that was belting down and they walked around the outside of the cottage and stood looking down on Lough Allen and said what a great view we had.

Then, they went into the office, the room with separate access adjoining the house, a single extension where I had worked for twenty-three years, writing books and plays and poems. A place where I had practised meditation for over a decade, going there each morning to kneel on the cold floor and light candles and incense sticks and worry my life away in that solitude that is called prayer.

The builders examined the office in silence: the dusty table, the dainty stove, as delicate as an hourglass, and the shelves of books. What occupied them most was the loft – a two-metre-deep shelf close to the ceiling supported by three four-by-four posts and painted in Tudor black.

One of them kicked the stove.

'That's only a toy, isn't it?' he said.

'No,' I said, 'it actually works.'

They stared at me.

'Sure it's grand,' one of them said. 'I suppose you'd get great heat out of it.' It felt like they were just humouring an idiot.

And then they turned to the loft. I'd built it myself after I'd returned from Mullingar in 2011. I bought four-by-four beams and six-foot planks and made a shelf half the length of the room. It wasn't good workmanship. The shelf sloped slightly and the uprights weren't quite straight, but it stored

183

twenty or thirty boxes of archival documents and drafts of old books or plays.

'Jesus Christ,' one of them exclaimed, 'who put that thing up?'

'I did,' I said.

'Right,' he said, 'sure it's grand.'

'Where do you want the wood from the office to go when we dismantle the loft?' one of them asked.

I said, 'It doesn't matter. You can throw it in the skip and take it away.'

'Fine.'

And away they went with hammers and crowbars, pulling the loft asunder and flinging it piece by piece out the door. It took them just under an hour or so to dismantle what I had spent three months trying to construct.

Then, they hefted in the heavy equipment – the jackhammers and drills and extension cables – and they plugged them into sockets and the extension leads lay criss-crossing the floor and they attacked the main wall between the office and the house, their mouths hidden by small white masks, their eyes covered by goggles and hard yellow hats on their heads in case anything fell on them.

It was a solid cottage, built in 1971 by the county council, and it took them the guts of the day to break through the wall and remove all the blocks. By 5 p.m. when they were packing the truck and the van and the Mitsubishi, I went into the bedroom and found a gaping hole opening into the office. A wound in the love nest where I had spent my life. A shambles in the place where the child's cot had once stood. There was dust covering the bed and the tall boy. The floorboards were ripped up where they met the wall and I could see the earth beneath.

The house was destroyed.

We used to have a carpet that I was proud of. I'd bought it for seven hundred punts in 1993. It was the most expensive thing in our little house. But, over the years, wine had been spilled on it and food trampled into it, and the dog spent five years farting on it, and the cat killed dozens of mice on it and ate their bodies and left their tails in the corner and under the sofa.

Sometimes, I would rush into the house with my boots on to see something on the television, like the day that Lady Diana died.

'Come quick,' the beloved cried. 'Lady Diana.'

I thought Lady Diana was on the phone.

I had been planting willows along the pathway to my studio and I rushed back up to the house and straight into the room.

'Take off your boots,' she said, half an hour later, when we had got over the shock of the young princess' death, so sudden and violent in a tunnel in Paris.

'Take off the boots,' she said again. 'Look at the carpet.' And she pointed to all the mud on the floor and on the boots.

Because we were proud of our carpet. And we wanted to take care of it.

I never imagined it being sliced in bits and taken away as the builders did on the second week in August 2015. And the stress of turning the house upside down was getting to me. I couldn't meet anyone eye to eye without crying. I was sleeping in the corner of the sitting room. I was whinging to the beloved that we should never have begun the renovations.

And she didn't disagree, because she had never pushed for an extension in the first place. In fact, she'd tried for months to tell me that she would be heading for Warsaw before it was finished.

'You don't want to be stuck with all this mess through the winter on your own,' she said. But I wasn't listening.

It only took them ten minutes to rip up the carpet, to cut it into pieces so that it was easier to roll, and then to take it out the door and onto the skip in the backyard. Ten minutes to strip the room down to floorboards that I had not seen in twenty-four years.

I might have tried to take it out in one piece and I would have been there all day. But the carpenters were skilled. They knew that rolling it up before getting it out the door was an impossibility. Instead, they simply sliced it up in portions and then it was no bother to roll up small sections and fling them out. One of them had worked in London for ten years. Who knows how many carpets he had cut up and thrown into skips along the sidewalks of Camden Town?

'It was hard over there,' he said, meaning England. 'The only thing people understand in London is that work is work.'

Right, I thought; work is work. Sounded like a hands-on attitude. As if it was the secret of the universe. Work is work. All I knew was idleness in the hills above the lake, a stove with the blazing fire and a bit of writing between the dozes. He knew different. He knew that work was work.

But, in the long run, his life was as futile as mine. Whether life was lived on the top of a high-rise building balanced on fresh planks of wood or in my studio churning out A4 sheets of windy sentences, it made no difference. The wooden floors of high-rise offices on the London skyline would hold no more trace of him than shredded paper blowing across some recycling tip would retain the scrawl of my own hand. When all is said and done.

When the floor had been laid in the front room they installed a new stove. And they installed a chimney box in the wall because, they said, you can't be too careful.

Then the painters arrived: three shy young men from Mayo. Sleepy boys with big eyes and white overalls, and I asked their permission every time I tried to make my way to the toilet, stepping over gallons of vinyl matt and ancient planks like the bones of a whale balanced between little step ladders so that the painters could get their rollers onto the ceilings.

I was only fit for bed. I wanted to lie down. And yet I couldn't because there were always people around, in the bedroom or the bathroom, with pencils in their ears and measuring rulers sticking out of their back pockets.

I was an outlaw in my own home. I would hide in the studio for hours and emerge when the workmen had gone. I would gawk at all they had done since morning, ripping up floors and chasing walls for electrical sockets and breaking in the ceiling to make shafts where the light could come down from the new windows in the roof.

189

I had committed an act of destruction, an act of violence on the narrative of our life. And it couldn't be undone. I didn't know how much the build was going to cost and I was too scared to ask and too terrified to share my financial anxiety with the beloved.

August was a wet month. We lived in a cloud of drizzle, but on the twenty-fourth the rain cleared. And all the rooms were wet with paint and slow to dry so it was time to make up a bed in my studio. If things had been normal, I would have gone to the green shed and taken out the lawnmower. But things were far from normal. I had nowhere to sleep. My beloved said she would sleep in the small bedroom. There was a single bed in there that the child had once used. But there was no room left for me. So I was forced onto a mattress in my studio.

The studio was a building that stood apart at the end of the garden with a vaulted ceiling and cross-beam rafters. Inside it was a mess: my iMac stood on the desk and a pile of dead computers were stored on various shelves. The stove was filthy with grime, and ashes overflowed from the box at the bottom onto the floor. There were books everywhere, in boxes, on the floor, on the windowsills and on shelves. There were ledgers for doing the accounts and boxes of documents, electricity bills, receipts and hundreds of early drafts of unpublished books I had been trying to write over the years. And everything tossed together in a private chaos. I pushed boxes of books out of my way and shoved documents into the corners as much as I could in order to open down a sofa bed and place the mattress on it.

I mooched around wondering if it was worth lighting the stove, but decided that since it was an August evening the Dimplex heater in the corner would be sufficient. My eye tried to avoid the mess on every shelf, the private letters strewn on the floor and jam jars with old biros and fountain pens as dead as doornails. Everything mocked me. All that stuff was me. My narrative. My life. My fountain pens. My manuscripts and ledgers and books. But none of it retained meaning. It was all the bric-a-brac of a bygone life. A moment ago. It was just a pile of shit: shit notes and shit memos and shit diaries. Newspaper cuttings with reviews of plays from thirty years ago. Photographs of a younger me at the Edinburgh Festival covered in grimy coffee stains, baby goo from a child who was now a grown woman and living her own life elsewhere. Everything yellowing with age and not of the slightest interest to anybody.

Hello Freddie

Early summer was a lovely time, just before I began to renovate the house. The beloved had come home. I was finished my theatre work. We had enjoyed a break in Donegal. And the new extension was still only a fanciful notion in my head. My studio might have been cluttered with shrines and icons and little gods, but I too had outgrown that sort of thing in the months after the show in the Gaiety.

I had been invited to participate in an event at the Borris House Literary Festival. A distinguished professor of philosophy from England and myself would engage in a public conversation. Professor Grayling was famous, erudite and all over YouTube in a white suit. What they were thinking when they invited me to talk with him I don't know, but I foolishly agreed and, in June, I was trying to prepare myself by reading his books every morning. I studied A.C. Grayling's ideas about God, or rather the absence of God, until I was blue in the face, bleary eyed and on the edge of sleep in my armchair.

I would doze for a while, and the book would drop from my lap to the floor, wakening me, and then I'd go for a walk to freshen up and rouse my brain to attention. The mind often went sluggish like that in Leitrim because I sat too long at the stove.

In the old days, long-haired artistic types would drive into the yard in rusting vans or Toyota Starlets, hoping for a leisurely chat, and I would open the door with delight because I relished those distractions.

A leisurely chat meant the entire afternoon in two armchairs. We'd hug the stove for heat, rolling cigarettes, looking out at the grey mist, talking about the meaning of life, the nature of love, the novels of Dermot Healy and why we were lucky enough to be living in Leitrim.

Of course we weren't lucky. We were artists who couldn't afford to live anywhere else. Bohemians who invaded the scrawny laneways and hilly roads in the 1980s, with infants dangling from every hip, in the hope of finding a cottage for three thousand pounds.

We sat in the rain for years, wondering if our children would evolve gills or bicycle pedals instead of feet, as we convinced ourselves that Leitrim would be paradise if only it wasn't raining and if only there were no midges.

By the time I got to Borris House, a grand mansion in beautiful parkland, on a warm Saturday afternoon in late June the festival was in full swing, the car park was full,

A.C. Grayling's lecture was booked out and I was terrified of the good professor.

He spoke in the main hall, which was packed with his many admirers. He spoke about God's absence, and how the idea of God was as absurd as if one were to imagine the local busman holding the reins of creation.

When someone asks the question 'Who made the world?', the conventional answer is: God made the world. But Dr Grayling pointed out that one might just as easily say Freddie did it. Because there is as little behind the word God as there is behind the random name Freddie. When we say God made the world, we are saying nothing more intelligent than if we were to say that Freddie made the world.

Would that satisfy us? Imagine if you wanted your child to get through their exams and you just said, 'I hope with the help of Freddie they will do well.'

Would that be enough?

Or if we were frightened by turbulence on a flight to New York or Warsaw would it be sufficient to say, 'We are in the hands of Freddie.'

And what about the doctor with the cancer patient who is nervous about chemotherapy. 'Don't worry,' the doctor might say. 'Everything will be OK. Just put your trust in Freddie.'

The examples eloquently illustrated to me how bluff hides behind the use of the word God.

Grayling didn't tolerate superstition or intellectual

laziness, both of which were deeply embedded in my personality, but, nonetheless, his lecture had a lightness and charm to it. Long haired and physically energetic onstage, he was truly very handsome and likeable. He didn't strut about or chew his words slowly in the affected manner of academics. He didn't ponder his sentences like some people do, as if they are amazed at their own intelligence. He spoke as if he were chatting about tennis or explaining the rules of cricket to young people.

And he didn't seem attached to the ideas he was offering about God and religion. He seemed to be just tossing them out for discussion: take it or leave it, this is my opinion.

Nor did he stick to philosophy. He touched on China and how dangerous that empire might be for the rest of us in the coming century. He spoke about recent scientific discoveries in relation to the brain, the possibility that determinism now has the upper hand in modern thinking.

And central to all his thinking was the need to let go of religious superstition.

But it's amazing how lazy my mind was. For years, I fell back on St Anthony to find the keys of my car. I kept filling in the scientific gaps with goddy woddy, no matter how many books I read by people like Dawkins and Grayling and others.

I was at the back of the hall, sitting on the floor because of the enormous attendance.

Reminding myself that I had come to the festival to

engage in a public conversation with him on the Sunday morning, I was now terrified.

Not just because I wouldn't be smart enough for a public debate but because he spoke with such authority. When he spoke about politics, I recognised that he was a much better person than me in his ethical approach to the world. He had courage. He was fearless in speaking out. When I heard him talk about the brain and science, I knew he was a more erudite person than me, and when I heard him recite poetry in fluent Chinese so that the music of his voice completely seduced the audience, I just felt, holy Jesus, the game is up. He was even more passionate than me. 199

I was angry with the organisers for inviting me to converse with him. Who the hell was I to be sitting on a stage with this fellow from Oxford? This world-class professor of philosophy? All I had was a BA from Maynooth. I was happy enough with it but I wouldn't be waving it in front of anyone's nose.

So I concluded that I wasn't capable of argument with him at all. I could only surrender. I could only love him for his many wonders.

The following day at 2 p.m. we met on the stage, shook hands and sat at opposite sides of a low coffee table. Each of us had microphones extended on long limbs that meant they were almost inside our mouths.

I guessed that it might be a good start to confess my confusion. So I explained that I was a rather shallow person and I presented him with some basic questions I had struggled with for years.

I said I had been a Catholic priest for a short while. And then I had practised Buddhism. And then I had suffered depression. And I didn't achieve very much when I was at university.

'So I am hardly a suitable person to argue with you,' I concluded. His arms were folded. His long hair flowed on either side of his face. He watched me over the rims of his glasses, perhaps waiting to see if I would pounce. Because he must be used to a lot of abuse from unconscious human beings who feel threatened when he challenges their superstitious faith.

'I have relied too much on ritual and religion for too long,' I declared, 'to get me through the day. I light candles and use incense and converse with mythic figures, and I know they are only mythic, but their icons adorn my walls.'

I told him I agreed with all he had said and wrote but what was I to do with the compulsive desires I had to fling myself before various religious images at regular intervals. I was simply asking for advice.

'How should someone like me move forward?'

He was kind in his answers and the audience enjoyed the intimacy of the exchange.

'We are both the same,' he said. 'You in your own way

are seeking the truth. Your quest and path are valid, though they are wrong.'

That stung my ego for a moment.

'Your truth is wrong,' he said, 'especially when you rely on certain forms of Buddhism, which are particularly superstitious. But nonetheless you are seeking truth and that is a good thing.'

I felt a bit flushed in the face when he said I was wrong. After all, there were two hundred people listening to us. So I said so.

'I'm a bit uneasy when you say I am wrong,' I said. 'That sounds very definitive.'

He said, 'I have an obligation to speak the truth. And if you are wrong, then I ought to say so.'

I accepted this as fair enough and we moved on, examining various aspects of religious faith and my naivety. Thus, we found a way of chatting like friends, and the audience relaxed and we had great fun. I had released myself from argument. From the possibility of knowing something. Because he was a teacher, a man who had devoted his life to achieving intellectual insight, I thought it was right for me to respect his clarity.

But it was his compassion that most impressed me. It was a subtle intellectual compassion that slipped out into the light every so often. For example, on one occasion we were discussing determinism: the predictability of the brain.

'When we are speaking of the brain,' I remember him

saying, 'we are discussing a certain aspect of determinism: the possibility that the body actually determines thought. Because we know that many thoughts arrive just after the secretions in the brain, the chemical activities that are associated with those thoughts. There is a link between the thought and the chemical event. But the most recent study suggests that the chemical event prefaces the thought.' I felt he was giving the benefit of the doubt to determinism. Then he added something entirely different.

'But the brain is not the mind,' he cautioned.

202 There was a pause, and I felt he had inserted an enormous distinction in a tiny phrase.

'And the mind,' he suggested, 'is what evolves with other minds. Or when we apply ourselves to learning and literature. The mind is changing within us and is changed by the experience of otherness, by learning and particularly by love.'

Fuck me, I thought. He's good. He's clear. Because, on the one hand, he could ably dismantle my constructs of religious faith and the hocus pocus of all my prayers. But, on the other, he was offering a possibility of the human mind as beautiful, surprising and loving.

So, on the one hand, he was a philosopher. And on the other hand he was more like a teacher of wisdom offering the same hope that Jesus or Buddha or most other great religious philosophers had offered down through the ages. Don't get caught up with the religious stuff at all. Just live fully in the present moment and love yourself and your neighbour and your enemy and, I suppose, in terms of Buddhism, your cat.

The stranger is always the next great possibility. Instead of locking myself away in solitude with garish idols, I should be embracing strangers. That's the wonder and simple message I took away from my meeting with Dr Grayling.

The hour onstage with him felt personal. It was like we were both in a room together on our own and he was my counsellor. I felt elated and liberated all of a sudden. Afterwards, we shared a pot of Earl Grey tea in the drawing room. He ate a biscuit and chatted with some admirers before rushing off to catch the minibus to the airport. I embraced him. And then he was gone.

203

Professor Grayling returned to me on that night in August. The house was upside down and I could not have remained in it, but I was also afraid to be alone in my studio. Afraid to look at the accounts for the year in case there was some mistake that would cost me money. Afraid that I might catch a cold. Afraid that if I left the heater on, I might not be able to breathe. Afraid that if I fell into a deep sleep, I might stop breathing altogether. Afraid there could be monsters waiting for me in the dreamworld. I might dream of priests beating me or strangers cutting off my hands and the dreams might be so intense that they would seem real.

I worried that the cat, whom I had seen earlier munching through scraps of chicken on the saucer outside my studio, might have swallowed a bone that would get caught in his gut and we'd have to bring him to the vet, and that would cost more money and my lovely black cat would die in agony.

But the anxiety continued to build as I paced the room. I went from one thought to another at such speed that I lost any sense of logic. Lost any context for my thoughts. I didn't know why I was thinking what I was thinking.

I started worrying about international wars. Weather. The prospect of rain. The guttering that was never fixed. The dead leaves in the water tank. And where the ladder might be. It could be anywhere. Someone might have stolen it. I hadn't seen it for months. Then there was the prospect of fracking and nuclear war and the surface of the earth turning to toast. And what about all the methane coming out of cow's arses? Who knows where that will all end?

When I drifted off to sleep, Professor Grayling came to me in a dream. I was on my deathbed and the professor appeared in a white suit and sat beside me and held my hand.

'Please, Professor Grayling,' I said, 'please tell me about the miracle of the loaves and the fishes again.'

The professor explained that it was very likely that the great multitude who had come to hear Jesus speak might have brought food with them. And some might have brought nothing. So when Jesus encouraged them to share, they did so and, as a result, all were fed, and there was still ample food left over. The only miracle was that people shared stuff with each other.

'Is that all?' I said to the professor. 'Is that all there is to it?'

205

'Yes,' he replied in the dream. 'That's all there is. The universe is empty. So fucking what?'

Each breath I drew seemed like it was going to be my last, until I woke up gasping for air.

But the reality was that all my gods were useless. All my Freddies were dead.

'Be, here, now,' a zen monk told me once. And I was. I was there, at that moment, and it wasn't pleasant. Going into the dark. Lying on the sofa bed. Waiting for things to get worse.

206 Afraid that if my mind warped any further, or if my perceptions of the world were distorted any further, I couldn't be sure of where I would end up or who I would become or what I would do. In fact, any human being is capable of despair as much as they are capable of hope. So who knows how someone drifts towards the abyss? Who knows how a person finds themselves on the edge of a cliff?

And how much of our lives is determined by chemicals and secretions of our brains? Perhaps the loneliest place of all is to be on the brink of the cliff thinking, not so much that jumping is a solitary act, but that jumping is the will of the universe unfolding. Jump, bitch, jump, dickhead, the cosmos may say to us in our moment of agony. As even Jesus cried out, 'My God, why have you abandoned me?'

When I was a child, I would wake up in the night, sweating and worrying that everyone had left the house and that I was alone. I would go downstairs and find that indeed there was no one else in the house. For one so young, the house was a vast universe and it seemed eerily empty without mother, who was perhaps gone to town on her bike to shop.

That's the sense I had in my studio: the world was an empty room. If I went outside, I thought, I would find there was no one else out there. And that kind of solitude was a dark place to be when I was a child but the feeling was no less terrifying at sixty-two years of age.

Earlier in the evening, when I had been dragging the mattress across the yard from the house, I'd seen a bird on the garden seat. She had looked at me. A big black feathered creature. From millions of years ago, the tiny remnant of her dinosaur mind had embraced me as I had looked at her. I'd seen her with my heart. A realisation rather than any knowledge of the bird. I couldn't even name her except to say that we were a grand pair of dinosaurs, me and her. She was exquisite in her own solitude and, for a second, I'd felt like I was walking into the studio to face something timeless and beautiful.

But that didn't last long.

Only the beloved remained as my refuge. She was like a compass. She kept me grounded. So rather than stay another moment alone, I decided to go and find her. I walked across the back yard and into the house to speak with her. I could explain to her that I was having a bad night. Tell her that the year had been too much. That I was carrying too much anxiety. That the building had got the better of me.

But I couldn't find her. She wasn't in the kitchen. She wasn't in the front room. And I didn't recognise the house as ours. It seemed different.

Ah yes, I thought, perhaps she has gone to Poland again. But no, she came back from Poland. What was I thinking? But then perhaps it was to SuperValu she'd gone. No? Why would she go to SuperValu in the middle of the night?

I rushed back outside and checked if her car was still at the gable wall. It was. I looked at my own car and opened

the door and sat into the driving seat. I heard the clunk of
the door closing. Then, suddenly, as I was staring at the
Mitsubishi logo on the steering wheel, I couldn't say where
I was. I couldn't say how I came to be sitting where I was. I
thought I was at a toll gate on the motorway. There must be
a queue behind me. There must be a cabin and a woman to
take the money. I looked in the rear-view mirror. I looked
around. Where the fuck was everybody?

And then it was over. I remembered where I was.

I remembered that the house was upside down. We had
builders in. Yes. Our bedroom had a gaping hole in the
wall. Which is why I couldn't find her. Of course. She was
in the child's room. I smiled and said, 'Yes, I'm OK now.'
And I was. I saw my face in the rear-view mirror. I could
remember everything again.

Although I knew that something had happened. I had
slipped for a moment into confusion, that space I remember
old men wandering in when I was a night porter in the
hospital and I'd find them on the corridors in pyjamas,
dragging catheters and urine bags behind them as they
looked for cows in a milking parlour that wasn't there. I
was neither ill nor old, and yet I had slipped my moorings
in the world and hadn't known where I was for that brief
moment. The world would never seem quite so secure
again. Ever.

I went back into the house and peeped in the door of
the child's bedroom. There she was, asleep. She looked

209

beautiful. I saw the universe regaining the solidity of its moorings through her. I could live and breathe through her. My mind was entangled with her. She was the door out of my solitude.

I remember a day long ago when we were young and she had long black hair and the empty rooms made our feet sound hollow on the floorboards and we spent all our money on Egyptian sheets. We'd thought about going to Italy forever. The eternity of a kiss. The fragrance of churches. The olives in a bowl on the tablecloth and the Cairo sheets drying in a warm breeze. And she ahead of me walking on the side of a dusty road and her toes in leather sandals and resting sometimes in the shade of a larch tree. Or spending nights listening to cicadas. The two of us with lamps in our hands. In the middle of Italy with a telescope. Making laughter out of darkness. Birdsong in the grey light of morning. We were artists by day, lovers by night.

When we were young we went shopping. Muesli and fruit and yoghurt were novelties. I claimed it was bad for her health. 'Too much roughage in the mornings is not good,' I said. Bad for the bowel. And I was always sucking oranges.

Sometimes I'd look up from my breakfast bowl at her as if, even then, I had lost my memory. I know because she would say it. 'What are you thinking of? You look like you've lost your memory.'

When we were young, she painted the house. Emptied the sink. Scoured the bath. I washed myself and bought a suit from the Oxfam shop and I took her to an Italian restaurant with orange walls.

Then in August 2015, my mind let go of all the names I had for things and I existed in complete uncertainty. I was afraid until I realised she was still there. I had an anchor in reality. A stranger who was dependable. Afterwards, I could hear the birds without protection. Their savage music poured into me as I left her sleeping in the house and came back out into open air. I was walking beautifully, slowly, barefoot, knowing that this was how to walk beautifully out of my anxieties. Which is what religion used to do for me.

It had been a pathway strewn with little gods that led me to a moment, exquisite and serene, where memory was erased and anxieties were forgotten and there was nothing. Everywhere.

We used to decorate the house at Christmastime with lots of trinkets and tinsel and coloured lights. And we put a string over the fireplace on which to hang cards and a tree in the corner was festooned with baubles and a crib underneath it. We bought the crib in Arizona in 1989, a straw roof on four pillars with tiny figures made of plaster. They had brown faces and black hair and were dressed in white, like Native Americans, and they stood around gazing at an infant in the straw.

The crib had always been very important for me. It was when I'd knelt down at the crib in our house in Cavan as a child that I had received my first intimations of a religious vocation.

I was in the hall of my parents' house just gazing at it. The figures of Mary and Joseph were more traditional back then and were reminiscent of nineteenth-century devotional paintings. I thought they were beautiful. I had a battery-powered torch which I moved around the roof of the crib, finding different angles and shifting the light inside the crib and composing shadows with the darkness and the light.

Then I sensed someone stepping down the stairs behind me on light feet. It could not be my mother because she was in the kitchen. It could not be my father because he was in the drawing room reading his paper under the light of the standard lamp. It could not have been my brother because he always came down the stairs like a galloping horse.

The figure moved down swiftly, before I could turn around, and I felt a hand on my shoulder and I knew it was an angel. I was afraid to look. I wondered if she was dressed in white feathers. Did angels even have a specific gender? For a moment, I imagined a masculine angel wearing a long black leather coat. And even though I wasn't sure what form the angel had taken, I sensed that it didn't really matter. The angel might have wings or lipstick or long, high boots, but I was certain that someone had come.

Someone had walked down the stairs and touched my shoulder. The hand of the angel touching me as I played with the crib and the little romantic sculptures of St Joseph and Mary were all simply God's first advance into my life. It was like someone whispering in my ear, 'Come follow me.' I felt goosebumps rise on the back of my neck. Then

I decided to turn around and look, but almost at that very same moment, the angel dissolved.

Later, I found this angelic presence surfacing in all sorts of unexpected places. Often when I was lying in bed, staring at the ceiling or out the window where, on summer mornings, the white clouds floated in the blue above the spire of Cavan Cathedral. I could feel the presence in the shade of trees, or by the lakeshore, or when I was clipping the hedge for my father one Saturday afternoon at about the age of eight and again I could hear someone whispering.

214

'Come away.'

This made me glad. Because it was delicious to be alive in this presence. To know, walking towards the school yard, worrying about canes and straps and all varieties of humiliation and punishment, that I was not alone.

As a child, I was allowed to serve Mass in the cathedral. And there too I could feel the presence when the bells rang at the consecration.

The priest was bent over the bread on the altar before me. I was knelt on the lowest step with my hands joined and I shook the bells, a kind of tiny brass umbrella of four small bells that tinkled just as the priest spoke the words of consecration.

'*Hoc est enim corpus meum.*'

The tinkling of bells was an angel's voice. I was certain of it.

When the choir sang in the gallery behind me, I could hear angels there too.

When I was in the senior class of primary school, I was taught by a saintly brother with a gentle voice, a soft smile and a compassionate heart. A brother who was not like all the rest and who frowned whenever we heard some of the other brothers roar at the top of their lungs in an adjoining classroom or when we heard them beating some unhappy child in the corridor for not knowing certain details of Irish grammar. Brother Joseph would shake his head and frown at the blackboard, sometimes leaning into it as if in despair, until the roaring stopped.

It was Brother Joseph who taught me to pray. He said that if we recited a certain prayer every hour of the day, then we would always be in the presence of God. Which seemed an amazing claim to me at the time. So I tried it.

'Let us remember that we are in the presence of God,' the brother intoned, every hour of the day, and the class fell silent.

I had delighted in pressing my lips to the edge of an icon in Bucharest, running my fingers along its surface as if it was the external shadow of something invisible. In the icon, I was reaching inwardly, towards a hidden part of my self.

I longed to be awake. For years, I had tried to escape anxiety and sometimes I succeeded in the great silence of devotion. Shoulder to shoulder sometimes in Buddhist retreat centres, with boys as lean as whippets or girls so intensely vegetarian and slim that if they swallowed a piece of apple I'd see it moving down inside them.

Sitting around on the floor of a house in Dublin with members of a Christian cult when I was seventeen, speaking in tongues and feeling as intimate as if we were all naked. Devotion had always been a stepping out of solitude.

Or in Maynooth when I met those beautiful young men in their black robes and hats, bearded and sallow skinned and groomed as perfectly as a raven's feathers, the world covered in snow and the three of us like brothers, moored and anchored to the icon in the room. We had walked the white fields under the frozen beech trees and had joked about the future and had promised each other the world, as young people do. They had teased me and said that Western culture was decadent, then they screamed with delight at *Top of the Pops*, saying that now they had seen the Devil.

The homemade lamp was always burning before the icon: a glass bowl full of oil and a small copper wire twisted across the top holding a length of string, which served as a wick, while we sat in silence.

In Bucharest, I'd had no hot water in my apartment and the bedclothes wouldn't satisfy a cat on a cold night, so I didn't wash or change my clothes for days. Outside it had snowed and the city was much like any other, with signs of destitution and isolation everywhere. One day, I saw an elderly man with blue fingers playing a violin on the street. I saw a woman sleeping on the grille that sucks warm air from the metro below.

But on the day I fled my apartment and booked a ticket home, I stepped inside a small little church of shadows – it was like finding a refuge from all the anxiety of the modern world outside. It felt like stepping again into the exquisite silence of the present moment.

But all that went pear shaped. My Romanian trip was a disaster. My tour and my playacting in the Gaiety brought me so close to the dark icon of the Bull McCabe that I was unnerved. I felt I was on the road to perdition. I went back to Leitrim and became a murderer of small animals with my strimmer and my lawnmower.

The magpies came close to the house. The robins looked in the window. A big hen thrush sat under a tree waiting for the berries to grow. They regarded me as the enemy.

Then I pushed for a new house, and that failed. The builders came and they remade my little paradise, but it was too late. I had already begun to spiral into chronic anxiety.

I had found a bleak refuge in solitude. I had entered and closed the door and I wasn't opening it again for anyone, not even the beloved.

At the end of August 2015, I hadn't much hope left in anything.

It's a wonder that I got past the noble professors in Maynooth in the late 1970s when I was studying for the priesthood. I could never quite get my head around their theology. On one occasion, I annoyed a young smooth-skinned intellectual lecturer with hair oil and aftershave by delivering him an essay with the title 'Was Jesus the second Eve?'

Besides, most of the professors in the seminary at that time were pedantic or cunning with an eye on their careers.

I suppose there were a few exceptions, like Professor Quinlan. An elderly gentleman, who, it was rumoured, had been dismissed from his post in an American university for siding with the anti-war protestors in the 1960s. According to other rumours, had been one of the first chaplains to walk into Auschwitz after the war.

In Maynooth, many students were intimidated by him because he became a furious conservative and spent an amount of time marching around the corridors in a foul temper, liable to sudden bouts of rage caused by random encounters with other human beings.

I would have expected to be eaten alive by him, except for the fact that he considered himself a poet. His extempore exegeses on the gospel texts in class were a riveting twice-weekly performance, when he would lean back in his chair, take the black spectacles from his bald and shiny head, look out the window and comment on the weather. As often as not, he'd begin with a few anecdotes about his grandmother in Kerry who, he implied, contained in her elderly Kerry skull all the wisdom of the universe and was never in need of reading the gospels in English.

I remember him advising us to avoid Beethoven's late quartets until we were over forty. On another occasion he spent an hour explaining why young men love spring and old men are fond of winter.

I followed his advice on many occasions and when I did open my heart to the late quartets in my forties, tears fell down my cheeks as I remembered him with a kind of love that a boy has for a man. I listened to them in winters when I suffered depression and felt as close to the old professor in those moments as when I'd stood before him long ago.

All these things came back to my mind on the night in August when my nerves snapped. When my icons died. When my hope and faith in anything personal about the universe crumbled.

I felt shame for my folly. Shame that I had been seduced by the Church. Shame that the Church had been so sleazy in its cover up of sexual crimes against children. Shame that I had never faced up intellectually to the facts. To the Grayling facts. To the Dawkins facts. To the facts of Auschwitz. Shame that while clutching my little gods, I had grown sour and selfish and mentally ill.

I felt angry for all the wasted years I'd spent sitting before icons that hung above small altars in quiet oratories. Anger at the desperation of all those devotees that sprinkle their faces in holy water as they bless themselves and think that a few moments before an icon might fix the universe for them. Couples in love, old men tasting widowhood, young nuns in search of ecstasy, pregnant women and elderly grandparents standing or kneeling in supplication that they might be winners in the grand cosmic lotto.

And fair play to my friends over the years who had tried to uncouple me from delusions that some great mother in the sky was holding me or that some heaven beyond this world was waiting for me. They may have known better than me that there is only silence beyond the grave. And that there are no cures for human isolation.

All those anxieties were bursting in me when, sometime after midnight, I found myself in my Mitsubishi ASX in the back yard, uncertain of where or who I was.

It was almost 3 a.m. when I returned to my studio. And I tried to put the events in sequence. Tried to remember where I was and what was happening.

Yes, they had opened the house with jackhammers a few weeks earlier. Yes, I had removed all my boxes of manuscripts and books and the bric-a-brac that had accumulated on shelves over the decades from the office and placed everything in the studio where I now sat.

My father's document box lay on the ground beside my feet. I opened it for no particular reason except to look at the documents again. But, this time, I saw something I had never noticed before. It was a silver medal lodged underneath an old envelope at the bottom of his papers. A silver circle containing the Star of David, and at the centre of the star I read the word 'Mazal' written in Hebrew letters.

I turned it over and over in my fingers for a long time as I put together the events of the day.

I had dragged a mattress across the yard to the studio earlier that afternoon. There it was in the far corner, on the opened sofa under the lamplight. The beloved had gone to sleep in the child's room. I had fallen asleep and dreamed of Professor Grayling.

222 Everything was as it should be.

Then sitting in the car, in a moment of exquisite forgetting, I had not known where I was. The bubble had burst.

Now I felt enormous relief. It was almost morning but I could neither sleep nor leave the room.

So I opened up my iPad.

When the Wi-Fi signal buffered and connected, I clicked the Periscope icon and a map of the world appeared, with red dots all across the continents indicating who was online. I surfed through America and waited for them all to appear on the screen: young people, with bongs and spliffs and cans of beer, sitting at make-up desks, powdering their noses, waiting for taxis, sitting on beds, playing with their pyjamas and all of them utterly bored. But at least they were there, on my screen, looking out at me. Of course, in their world they were looking at their own iPhones, gazing into a dark universe like Alice at her mirror; except that I, and perhaps a few dozen other peeping Toms, were behind their mirror, gazing back at them.

Little texted questions floated up the screen from the other viewers. One girl was smoking a bong and she brought us around her flat, which was a terrible mess of clothes scattered on the floor and a disorganised bundle of make-up pencils and tubes lay on her dressing table. She took us outside the room and down a corridor where a sleeping dog didn't even bother to move his head in acknowledgement of her.

223

She must be very low in the pecking order if even the dog doesn't bother with her, I thought.

And then back in her room, she swallowed another cloud from the bong and another question floated up on her screen.

'You have a volcano on your forehead,' someone texted, referring to a large, ugly blue pimple above her eye. She rubbed the pimple but said nothing, like a child might do when they have been shamed.

'Were you ever raped?' someone else texted. The question shocked me. And so did the answer.

She said, 'Yes,' as if she was compelled to answer. 'I was raped twice.'

Why are you telling this to a stranger? I wondered. And I could only guess that she was terribly lonely.

Which is what made her matter to me.

My icons were not lonely. My great-grandmother on my iPhone was not lonely. Not even Jesus was lonely. But here was a real person, broken and alone. And she was present, at least on the screen. Maybe as time goes on, that's as good as it gets. They were all real. From the trailer parks of LA to the apartment blocks in Minsk.

I could surf, and select and watch and they became present to me.

I stared back at the Periscope kids for ages, switching from parks in California to various housing estates in Finland and Belarus, and it was always the same. Even though I didn't speak Russian, I could figure out what they were saying.

But it calmed me. It was relaxing to hear their stories.

I searched the drawers until I found a little white plastic machine for measuring blood pressure. I strapped it to my arm and pressed the buttons and waited for the digital brain to do its job. In a few moments, the numbers flashed and changed and then finally with a bleep the machine declared my pressure. It was perfectly fine. I was chilling out.

So back to Periscope.

The girl on the bong with the pimple was still talking from her squalid bedroom in Los Angeles. I wished I was with her and I texted: 'I hope you are having a good day.'

I could see her reading the text and then she said, 'Ah, thank you. Thank you, Michael.'

That was amazing – to hear her speak my name on the other side of the magic mirror out there in America.

'Thank you, Michael.'

Goddy woddy never spoke to me like that.

So I remained for hours in that sad, uneasy world of strangers whispering at me on the pillow. Young people from all over the world, glued to their screens, hoping that someone was listening. Although most had only a handful of viewers. And the texts to them were never interesting and often abusive.

'Show us your boobs,' someone would text.

'Fuck you, nigga.'

'Your hair is nice.'

'Smoke on the scope.'

'Show pussy.'

I saw a young woman in Utah. By then, it was 5 a.m. but for the woman in Utah it was only 10 p.m. the night before.

The sheets were white and her nightdress was white but she was fully made up in red lipstick and dramatic mascara and eyeliner. She had been out to dinner with her man and she had had a bad time so she'd come home. Obviously, she threw herself in the bed without cleaning her make-up and now she was online telling me what had happened.

Apparently her boyfriend had flown from Texas to be with her, but when they went out to the restaurant, he bought another girl a drink at the bar.

That finished her. She couldn't cope.

'He's an asshole,' she said. 'A fucking asshole. Buying some other bitch a drink. I mean, what the fuck did he fly up from Texas for if he was going to insult me like that in front of all the motherfuckers?'

I wanted to tell her he wasn't really insulting her. He was just buying a drink for someone else.

But I said nothing.

Instead, I flipped over to Angelina, a cool girl in Los Angeles whose broadcasts I followed regularly. She was smoking a bong and her determination to suck every shred of smoke up the funnel of the bong alarmed me. She had a fierce dry cough.

Every time I looked, she was smoking something different, and she said online that she was only seventeen.

I was wondering, What the fuck does her mother think of this?

But even her mother appeared once on the screen and she didn't seem to give a fuck what her daughter did. She was a cool mom, and the kitchen was as big as our cottage, with an island in the middle and pots hanging from the walls, and when Angelina said she wanted the keys of the car to go into town, her mother just tossed them across the worktop, and Angelina headed out the door with the phone in her hand so I could join her for the trip downtown in a big blue beast of a jeep to find herself some more drugs.

Angelina thought she was talking to someone. Someone out there. The number of viewers she had was signalled at the bottom of the screen. But it only signalled one. All she had was me.

People on Periscope think they can turn on the phone and connect with the otherness of the universe. The mysterious others who are there and who might love them.

They sit at their little mirrors, confessing their secrets to the dark cosmos that watches us all.

227

In fact, it even seemed a bit like prayer, as they attempted the impossibility of reaching out to some life beyond the screens of their phones.

'Can't sleep', Angelina declared in a text that reached all her followers, including me the following morning at 9 a.m. Irish time, when the summer sun was slanting in through the kitchen window and cutting the face off me as I tried to eat my muesli in the chaos that the builders had made. But Angelina was still in the dark, drowsy and sad, coughing into the Californian night.

I watched her clean the bong, load the bong and smoke the bong. I watched the abusive texts scroll up over her body.

I wanted to reach into the screen and take her out of her life and put her sitting on the sofa like a cat and tell her I would mind her.

'Did you have a rough night?' the beloved enquired as I kept my nose stuck in the screen of the iPhone.

'Not too bad,' I replied. I didn't say more because the builders were sawing through the ceiling above our heads to make a skylight and the dust was falling on my muesli.

The beloved didn't know what was going on inside me because I didn't tell her. I kept everything to myself.

At the end of September, she went away to Warsaw to work at the National Museum, making a copy of the *Icon of Kazan*, a precious medieval object that is housed there. She worked in conjunction with the Academy of Fine Art and with some assistance from an extraordinary icon maker and artist from Belarus. She left in September and returned nine months later, in June 2016. For most of that time, I was in Leitrim, spending my days at the fire. I had simply burned out again after too much anxiety. Overloading myself with work. So I decided to rest for the winter, although the anxiety that caused a severe panic attack in August didn't get much better.

Looking back, I felt everything had been leading to that moment in August, when I went out to sleep alone in my chaotic studio. All that solitary travel from one venue to another during the winter, all those performances in the theatre that had raised my anxiety levels more and more each week, and all that manic rage that began to erupt in me when I was working in the garden: it all came home to roost in my studio on that August night.

Afterwards, my body began breaking down, too. Over the following three months, I could feel a volcano of stress in my bones and my gut and the back of my neck.

I developed pain in the heel of my foot. I could barely walk. I hobbled into the doctor's surgery one afternoon and was told it sounded like plantar fasciitis but, the doctor added, it could also be the result of worry and overwork. 'Have you been under any stress lately?' she asked.

'Not at all,' I lied. 'No stress.'

I googled 'plantar fasciitis' to increase my misery and I went to Foot Solutions in Galway, hardly able to keep my foot on the accelerator pedal of the car because of the pain, and I bought shoes for €350 in the hope that they would help.

I began noticing a flashing light in my right eye, like fireworks, every time I moved my focus and two floaters drifted across my view of the world like tiny hairs. Sometimes a black veil, like a fingerprint would drift into view. The doctor sent me to an ophthalmologist. She said it might be a sign that the retina was detaching from the back of my eye because of age or macular degeneration.

But I knew it was stress.

I developed a stiff shoulder and I couldn't write for weeks – on a number of occasions, I had to withdraw from my column in the newspaper. I went to a physiotherapist in Carrick-on-Shannon every week and lay on a table as he tried to squeeze the tension out of my muscles. But it got worse and I couldn't look sideways.

I went back to the doctor, still hobbling in my expensive shoes and now unable to turn my head sideways.

The dispensary had a bright waiting room and an office for the receptionist, and there were two rooms down the corridor, where the doctors sat behind clean desks with their laptops and stethescopes at the ready, and their desks stacked with folders of intimate notes about patients' bodily functions.

I sat in the corner of the waiting room, facing two other invalids. One was an elderly man with shaking hands, thick glasses and a chalk white face. A bloodless old fellow like someone who has long ago renounced the pleasures of the world and retired to the solitude of his own psyche to become more spirit than flesh – a kind of living abstraction.

The other was a little woman with a red face. She had a handkerchief the size of a small towel on her lap, which she moved from hand to hand and when necessary to her nose.

There was a talk show in full swing on the wireless that sat on a ledge outside the secretary's office.

The radio is an important device in any doctor's surgery.

It keeps people who might know each other from falling into idle chat about their private ailments because, in rural Ireland, the body is an absolutely isolated universe. The radio also creates a kind of serenity in the waiting room akin to a singing deacon in a church.

The radio presenter was talking to a sex therapist and reading out problems that listeners had texted or emailed in.

Apparently someone in their sixties, who was having sex four or five times a week up until recently was now experiencing a downturn, and was worried that once a week was an unnaturally low performance level.

'What should he do?' the presenter asked the therapist.

I tried to distract myself with other thoughts. I tried to think of thrushes that had arrived in the garden that morning and were feeding under the trees. But I couldn't resist looking at the old man opposite me. For all I knew, he may have had a wonderful sex life. He may have performed for years on a daily basis with sudden grace endlessly surprising his beloved, like a little hawk that swoops with elegance on his little hen. But there was no trace of any such adventures left in his body now.

The therapist on the radio was explaining that sometimes orgasms can be hard to achieve and that sometimes sexual pleasure is about more than just an orgasm. This caused the little fat lady to sneeze a huge cloud of wet germs into her handkerchief and, in an aftermath of devastating chest movements, she coughed up phlegm which her handkerchief swallowed as it emerged from her mouth.

'Does it take him longer than normal to ejaculate?' the therapist asked. 'It may simply be an issue of ageing.'

I looked at the old woman and the man opposite me and wondered when was the last time either of them had been on fire with desire. It occurred to me that everyone in the world must eventually arrive at what turns out to be 'The Last Orgasm'.

'Does he wear glasses?' the therapist wanted to know. It sounded like an accusation, and I was slightly relieved that I had left my own glasses in the car.

The little lady smiled across the room at me as if we were all children listening to a fairy tale and I was glad when the secretary called my name and I went down the corridor to the surgery.

I met the General one day for lunch in Dublin, although I took the train rather than driving because I had put two dings in the rear end of the Mitsubishi the previous week by reversing into walls. A sure sign that my anxieties were spiralling.

I met the General at Connolly. He had a taxi lined up to take us to a restaurant in Dún Laoghaire.

'You're crippled,' he said as I hobbled towards him. When he helped me into the taxi, he said that he insisted on paying for the meal.

I had a voucher for a unisex beauty therapy centre which I'd got at Christmas and it was almost out of date. I told him he was welcome to it, that they did waxing.

The word caught his attention.

'Waxing?' he said. 'But my ears are perfectly fine.'

'I think it's the other end they would be waxing,' I said.

He stared at me until the penny dropped.

'Ah,' he said, 'I see,' and he slipped the voucher into his breast pocket and muttered something about how desperately men need a woman's touch.

'Why don't you use it yourself?' he asked.

'Are you fucking joking?' I replied. 'I'm crippled. My nerves are in flitters. How could I possibly lie on a couch and allow anyone tear out my pubic hairs? Do you think I'm a complete masochist?'

The Sligo train can be a kind of refuge after a day in the city. People board half an hour before the train leaves just to get a good seat. Young girls use their phones to tell their mammies where they are, and women phone husbands to make sure they'll be picked up at their station. Everyone nibbles at dainty muffins or chocolate bars bought at the kiosks in the station.

There was a man sitting opposite me with prominent teeth and a smile that implied a degree of bewilderment. He stared at me silently until we were beyond Maynooth. Looking out the window at the spire that rises above the trees in the old seminary, he leaned towards me and spoke. 'I've been on retreat this week.'

I nodded.

'It was fantastic,' he continued. 'Buddhists, vegetarians, yoga teachers and a lot of young women. We were practising compassion all weekend.'

'Well, that's good,' I said.

'Yeah,' he said, his bewildered smile still in my face, and his eyes glued to me. 'We were learning how to be compassionate to the vegetables.'

I was tempted to stare out the window and ignore him, but, after a pause, my curiosity got the better of me.

'How do you practise compassion with a vegetable?'

'Well, first,' he said, 'they told us to peel a carrot very slowly with a peeler. And then they asked us to imagine how the carrot felt.'

'Who do you mean by "they"?' I asked.

236

'The Buddhists,' he whispered, as if we were in an episode of *Doctor Who* and Buddhists were evolved Daleks.

'Just imagine you're a carrot,' he went on. 'That's how they do compassion – they imagine what it's like to be the other person.'

'Or the other carrot,' I added.

'Yeah,' he agreed with the sincerity of a man whose soul has been rinsed clean of irony. 'You imagine you're the carrot and you get an idea of what it might be like if the blade was peeling your skin off.'

'And what happened then?' I wondered.

He paused.

'We had dinner,' he said. 'Beef stew. With potatoes and onions. And carrots.'

Now we both looked out the window.

'What's the book?' he asked, looking at *A Small History of Icons* on the table between us.

'It's just a history book,' I said.

'Icons,' he said with a sneer.

'Yes,' I repeated, 'icons.'

'Icons,' he repeated.

'Yes,' I repeated. 'It's a book.' I would have loved to slap him in the face with it.

'Very interesting,' he muttered and lifted the book, glanced at the image and put it down again. 'Although personally speaking,' he added, 'I think I've outgrown that sort of thing.'

I thought I, too, had outgrown that sort of thing, although sometimes I tried to recover what I had lost, to reclaim the calm abiding of mind that I had enjoyed over the years as a fruit of religious practice.

But it didn't work. All I had to cling to in the end were Xanax tablets and live feeds from Periscope.

I returned to my therapist, going to see her every two weeks. I went to an acupuncturist every Wednesday. And I tried to rekindle the practice of meditation.

But fundamentally, I was alone. I shuffled around the house talking to myself. And I know that it was foolish not to have told my beloved. Not to have shared my distress. Foolish not to have gone with her as she had suggested.

I suppose men are a merry little bunch of pioneers in the dark who get more cheerful the more grim the weather becomes, and who can cycle on flat tyres for miles without admitting that their bum is in flitters. There's nothing as funny as pure misery to a man's mind, and he can often walk over a cliff while making jokes about how he never learned to swim.

Sometimes, I ventured out for lunch, in Drumshanbo, Cavan or Mullingar, just for the sake of a brief human exchange with the waiter or the person at the till in a carvery restaurant. I saw other men alone, or in little bunches, sustaining themselves with humour in the bleak dark that was all around them.

Two old boys in the Kilmore in Cavan were talking of fish one day.

'Did you do any fishing this weekend?' the bespectacled one enquired.

'Killykeen on Saturday morning,' the lean one replied, as he chewed roast beef like a hungry whippet.

Then, he stopped chewing, for dramatic reasons, and stared at the bespectacled one. 'There were nine Dutch fellows along the shoreline under the wooden bridge. *Nine*,' he stressed, holding up four fingers of his left hand. 'Nine. Fucken mental. How could you catch a fish with that crowd?'

'Did you catch anything?' the man with the glasses asked.

'I did,' the whippet replied. 'Just the one. But he was hardly as big as me mickey.'

On a few other occasions, I went to Mullingar, hoping to lunch in the Greville Arms. One day I saw Tommy, an old friend, alone at another table.

On his way out, he touched my wrist as he passed. 'Good to see you back in Mullingar.'

He was almost gone, but I stopped him.

'Tommy,' I said, 'it's great to see you, really great,' exaggerating a little, because that's what lonely people do.

And he, being encouraged by such enthusiasm, said, 'Do you mind if I sit down?'

'Please do,' I replied.

He sat and we began to talk almost immediately about human tragedies and global disasters and the deaths of people we knew, which is Tommy's favourite subject.

'Did you know that they've opened a crematorium in Cavan?' he said.

'No,' I replied, 'I didn't know that.'

'The flame in the furnace is situated just underneath where the deceased's heart is because that's one of the most difficult bits to burn. Did you know that?'

'No, I didn't.'

'And afterwards,' he continued, 'they crunch the bones in a machine so that the ashes don't contain lumpy bits.'

When I was leaving, I embraced him and said he was a tonic and that it was really good talking to him. He *had* cheered me up, but it was strange that I could not tell him how wretched I felt.

After that, I made a determined effort at meditation. The days were shortening and the mornings were dark and, yet, one morning, I woke before dawn and went to the bathroom, washed my teeth and splashed hot water on my face without switching on a single light. Then I took a jug from the shelf and filled it with well water from the bucket by the back door and went outside. The moon was still in its first quarter. I stood for a moment gazing at it. The jug of well water was my offering.

I walked across the back yard to the studio. I opened the sliding glass doors and went inside, taking off my shoes, crossing the floor in stocking feet and holding the jug of water. I sat on a cushion. I put the jug on the floor.

I poured water into seven water bowls. I took charcoal from a container and held it over the flame and then spread incense on the charcoal. The flames illuminated the walls. I joined my hands and prostrated my body.

I stretched on the floor as shadows danced on the wall and a pale light of morning edged above the mountain beyond the lake.

I lay for a long while.

'Fuck it,' I said eventually, out loud, and I rose from my knees. 'Fuck it. I'm finished with this.'

It was the end of my search for samadhi.

I went immediately to the Periscope icon on the iPad and clicked on a rapper in Chicago who sat on his doorstep swallowing clouds from a bong and talking to his five other viewers about what a happy person he was, and I wanted to reach into the screen with my finger and touch his wretchedness.

240

Igloos in the Air

Even if the beloved had been in the room, I would not have shared this with her. A wall had come down around me. When I spoke to her on FaceTime or Skype in the evenings, I was frozen before the camera, stiff as a poker on the edge of the couch.

I had nothing to report apart from the fact that it was raining or not raining, and that I had fed the cat or not fed the cat.

She didn't realise what was happening. I'd bottled it inside from the moment she'd walked out the door and left me standing there, smiling.

I spent all winter in the half-made house with a hole in the wall and a huge empty hole in my gut, where God used to be. I sat by the fire for months and nothing but sorrow came each evening with the encroaching dark. I tried to read books but I read without concentrating. I read five pages and couldn't remember a word.

Sometimes, I stopped reading and turned on audiobooks or found a philosopher on YouTube and thought that if I immersed myself in the ideas of Dawkins, Grayling or other philosophers or scientists then I would not be so immobilised, in bed crying for hours each morning or breaking down in the evenings when I heard Rachmaninov's *Vespers* on Radio 3.

As I approached December, with Xanax tablets in my wallet, I hoped the crisis might end because the beloved would be home for two weeks at Christmas

244   I turned on the lights of the Christmas tree one evening, a tattered and uneven cluster of dead branches which I had robbed in the forestry the previous day. The needles were dropping fast. I could hear them softly falling through the air to the floor and I sat listening, as if to a ghost.

I had a chicken in the oven, roasting on a tray of carrots and potatoes. I took the tray out and ate by the fire. My hand was shaking. It had been happening on and off for weeks, usually when I took up a knife or fork.

Sometimes, I checked my body. That's what the therapist had told me to do when I was getting immobilised by stress. Check the body. Pay attention to each single limb and bone, from toe of foot to hair of head. Then by stretching out my arms and carving a space in the air all around me and above my head, like a small igloo, I named my boundary. I claimed the space around me as mine.

My therapist advised me to do this when I felt

overwhelmed by negative emotions. All my troubles stemmed from being forgetful about boundaries, she suggested. Allowing people to invade my space had been my downfall as a child. And whenever I did a few stretches, I felt the autonomy of my body return.

'I am here,' I whispered. 'I am here alone by the fire with my roast chicken on this dark winter night.'

But my hands were shaking. My great-grandmother was looking at me from the wall. I think she was horrified.

I ate dinner and, once again, carved my igloo in the air, like a barrier, and I sat back in the chair and saw a robin sitting on top of a flowerpot just outside the patio door. The bird was staring at me, as if he wanted my attention.

It was already dark. It was only by the light on the outside porch that I could see him. What such a creature was doing at the window after dark I could not tell. Although after a while I noticed that my hands had stopped shaking.

While playing the part of the Bull McCabe in the Gaiety Theatre, there was one scene more than others which I dreaded. It was when the Bull kills the stranger, on the stage, in despair and the fog of night.

In the wilderness of the field, the Bull raises his eyes to heaven after the deed and cries out to the dead stranger who lies at his feet.

'Why couldn't you stay away, you foolish boy?' he cries, 'Look at the trouble you drew on yourself.'

When I looked up and outwards from the stage, I saw a startled audience in both balconies and in the gods and in the stalls. I had just killed someone. They felt it. All the other actors had fled the scene, fled the stage, and I was alone; I was the Bull in his moment of guilt and remorse.

And no remorse is as pure as that which is experienced alone. When there are no lovers or companions or fellow travellers to soothe the pain. No therapist, shaman or priest to advise a person how to breathe or make igloos in the air or read books.

What have I done? the Bull wonders.

Everyone wonders. Everyone asks, 'What have I done?'

Maybe that's the question that makes us human.

Whenever I did venture out of the house in an effort to connect with other people, I felt remote from them and disjointed from the narrative of their lives.

I made a trip to Dublin and was standing at the window of Hodges Figgis when I saw the full text of 'Sailing to Byzantium' by Yeats in the window.

The older I get, the more I understand the poem. The unease of an old man, being in a country where the young are slapping their delicious skins against each other in a frenzy of passion and where an old man is nothing more than a tattered coat upon a stick.

I have great sympathy for Yeats, who went to such trouble to achieve sexual arousal late in life, submitting himself to an exotic vasectomy in order to raise his libido. I've read accounts of him stalking a young woman at a public lecture and inveigling himself into her car and sitting with her for hours as she sang the praises of a younger man. That must have been sore on the old goat.

As I was thinking of Yeats, I saw the General farther up the street and we walked around the corner in search of coffee and walnut cake and I told him about my reflections on Yeats.

'Maybe he never heard of chillies,' the General suggested. 'That's the stuff that can awaken the libido into pulsating flesh.'

We were sitting in the sun at a restaurant table on Duke Street.

I asked him how many chillies I would need to consume in order to get a libidinous buzz.

'You don't eat them,' he said dismissively. Then he leaned over the table to me so that no one could hear. He whispered his instructions for the use of chillies into my ear and then leaned back in his seat, his eyebrows extending halfway up his forehead.

I laughed.

'No laughing matter,' he said. 'I got the advice in Arizona in July from a medicine man, a long-haired Caucasian who was wearing more turquoise rings and necklaces than an extra in a John Wayne movie. Nevertheless he had a PhD in sexual therapy.'

'What were you doing in Arizona?'

'Visiting the children,' he said.

'You don't have children in America,' I said.

'That's beside the point,' he replied, 'but I did meet a wonderful young lady in Phoenix who practises shamanic

249

healing. It was thirty-five in the shade and she said I should go see the medicine man because of my problem. The medicine man turned out to be from California. When I came back with the chillies, she asked me if I wanted to try them and I said I did. Before I knew it, I could feel a sensation in my groin like a rod of lightning. In fact, the only problem was that the pain became so intense that we had to cancel coitus for the evening and she got little bottles of iced water from the fridge to cool me down.'

The waitress came to take our order, a slim woman with dark hair.

250

'The Caesar salad looks good,' I said to the General.

'I thought you said we were going to have walnut cake,' he protested.

'Oh, we have walnut cake also,' the waitress said.

'The salad would be healthier,' I suggested.

'Walnut cake,' the General insisted, pouting at me, and so I agreed.

When it arrived, we consumed it with spoons and the General continued on the subject of Arizona for a long time, singing the praises of various therapies he had been lured into during the summer.

Then he remembered that he was meeting someone at the Abbey Theatre at 7 p.m.

'Chillies,' he whispered as he stood up to go. 'Chillies are the secret that Yeats never found.'

'Enjoy the theatre,' I said.

'There's more to life than Caesar salads,' he snapped, as he turned on his heel and walked away with his chest puffed out like a pigeon and his rear end trailing behind him.

When he was gone, I sat with the dregs of my coffee until the waitress came to clear the table. Suddenly, the phone in her pocket rang and she dashed into the street to answer it. But she looked sad when she put the little phone to her ear. I suspect it was her lover on the other end. She listened most of the time, apart from a few interjections.

'Yes.'

'I see.'

'I understand.'

'Well that's OK.'

She too seemed uneasy and remote from the life going on around her. She replaced the phone in the pocket of her apron and, with a sense of quiet dejection, went back inside the restaurant, without even remembering to take the empty plates from which the General and I had recently gorged on walnut cake.

That evening, I was glad to be back in the safe environment of my trees. My wilderness of rustling leaves and black cats. Even though the trees were withered in the winter twilight, the birch and oak, the weeping and the frugal willow, the mountain ash and the wild cherry were almost bare in the bleak November dusk.

The laburnum was choked with lichen and a pagoda tree, overwhelmed by shadows beneath the oaks, was dying. Only the Chilean beech trees, gigantic hardwood evergreen warriors that reached into the sky beyond all others and towered over the little cottage, were green and lively in the wind.

I strolled about admiring my little forest, trees I had planted in the very same year that Radovan Karadžić wiped out nine thousand boys and men in Srebrenica and all those trees were blooming still, innocent and lovely, and all those boys were dead.

The picture of Martha caught my eye as it always did when I entered the house and put on the lights.

I wondered if she'd felt at home in Pembroke Cottages in Dublin, when she'd first crossed the threshold with her husband or had she felt at home later in Beaver Row, where she'd grown old and died. Had she felt at home or had she longed for some small village in the forests of Poland that nobody knew about and whose name she took with her all the way to her grave in Dundrum?

254 On another dark and wintery day in mid-December 2015, I went to Cavan, just to check on my mother's house that had been standing empty for three years.

Afterwards, I decided to pick up some meat in town and as I was standing at the butcher's counter trying to make up my mind between a spicy sausage or a single lamb chop, the butcher started looking at me like I was an old cow that might have to be put down.

'You're not yourself,' the butcher said.

'It's the time of year,' I replied.

'I know what you mean. Sure it gets to us all, doesn't it?'

'It does indeed,' I agreed. And I added, 'I'll have a half pound of the spicy sausages and three lamb chops,' because I didn't want the butcher to know that my beloved had gone and I was alone.

The butcher didn't specify what gets to us all, but there is a general acknowledgement that the winter is a time when melancholy can turn to depression and the doctors' surgeries of the country fill up with people looking for tablets.

Nobody likes to talk about depression in real life. It's only on the radio that it sounds heroic. So it's called other things.

'I get a touch of it myself,' the butcher said, as he handed me a brown parcel of meats. 'Maybe it's just loneliness.'

I suppose that the words change but the experience remains the same. For me, the melancholy of winter manifested as an inertia in my limbs so that eventually my days were reduced to little more than feeding the cat. I got exhausted by even a single task.

The only consolation was to acknowledge that there were more than me suffering. Hundreds of weary souls scattered across the countryside. I could recognise them everywhere, walking the streets of Cavan and Mullingar or standing at bus stops in Dublin. Sorrow caused by age, or a broken leg, or a chronic illness, or the unresolved stuff that went on years ago with some heartless parent – the result was always the same. People walking across Ireland in the early-evening twilight of December with weary steps or struggling to get to the kitchen and make themselves a cup of tea. The trembling hands of creatures being devoured by disturbing emotions.

Many people talk about battling depression. Like a poet I met once who told me that depression was like a flock of crows. We were in a bar in Dublin. The poet had just had an

255

argument up the street with his partner and he was nursing a pint. He always looked like a man who never slept.

'Depression arrives like a flock of crows sometimes,' the poet said. 'But you must never let them sit,' he warned, and he dug his finger into my shoulder. He was that kind of poet. He'd tell you how to eat your dinner.

And he spoke with fear in his eyes like a man in a shed waiting with his gun for the enemy to arrive. The more the poet struggled to scatter the melancholy, the more it took hold of him in other ways.

256 But I could never endure that war. I just surrendered to the sadness and went to bed. Accepting depression was like allowing my entire body fall into an ocean without knowing how deep it might be or how far into the night the tide might carry me.

That autumn, I tried to allow the melancholy and sorrow and grief to roll over me. It often arrived in the evenings with the fading light at 3 p.m., and I would fly to the bed, cherishing the safety of pillows or the music of Scriabin seeping up from the speakers beneath the bed.

I felt alive in the pain. It was as if I held myself in existence. And it was as if, outside the window someone else was holding the trees. And someone else held the dark and ragged crows. Some invisible ground of being held all those things together, I thought, because they are given. They appeared before me as miracles to be processed. Then the crows came closer. And I welcomed them. And we all slept together, briefly free from the strange anxiety of being. All that clinging clinging clinging – to the beloved and goddy woddy, to gods and little icons in the dark – was peeling away. I was naked emotionally, and the obvious indifference of the universe was comforting. The more I looked at the trees in the garden, the more I felt reassured that dying was natural. There was nothing to fear.

One day, the postman stopped his van and saw me in the kitchen, so he came to the window and knocked on the glass.

'Well, how was the year for you?' I enquired.

'Ah, you know,' the postman said, 'some years can be a nightmare. But what can we do? You take it as it comes. Isn't that right? You have to let the universe unfold.'

He was holding a bunch of white envelopes, Christmas cards, fliers for supermarkets and a lumpy parcel. I was holding a box of chocolates wrapped in red Christmas wrapping paper.

'We had fifteen extra trays today,' the postman said. 'Imagine that. Fifteen. Just today alone.'

I didn't know what that meant, though I suspected an extra tray of mail was a big deal for the postman to sort and deliver. Not to mention fifteen extra trays.

'You must be flat out for Christmas,' I said.

'Don't be talking about it,' the postman replied. 'Imagine, fifteen trays.'

'So when do you finish up?' I wondered.

'I should be all done by lunchtime on Christmas Eve,' the postman said. 'I hope. You'll see me flying up this road like a bat out of hell on my way home. Hopefully.'

I passed the box of chocolates out the window. The postman was surprised.

'It's just a token,' I said. 'To say how grateful I am for all your help. Because if I'm not in the house and you arrive with a parcel you always leave it in the shed and then write a little note on one of the other envelopes so I know. That's a great help to me. I really appreciate it.'

258   The postman was young and eager to oblige. He spoke unconsciously but he was wise in ways that postmen often are.

'Some years are a nightmare,' he said.

I agreed.

'But maybe 2016 will be better.'

In Dark Times

And so the beloved came home for two weeks, and I kept to myself, and we went to a hotel for Christmas Day, with a wide family group. I was no longer thinking about my great-grandmother or my good neighbour or anyone else who had departed. Time moves on and everyone is forgotten. I was OK with that. I had come to the end of my prayers. I had nothing further to worship. I saw the trees for what they really were: just trees.

I went to my mother's grave and put flowers on it on New Year's Eve, but I just stood there, observing the wet clay, the cold stone, the indifferent gothic calligraphy that summed up her life: 1916–2012. I spoke to no god and met no angel as I walked back to my jeep. And I drove away in the bleak mid-winter twilight as all the dead lay easy in the clay behind me.

No one mentioned our departed neighbour over the Christmas holiday. He had already fallen into obscurity.

Although on one occasion my daughter was staring at the photograph of Martha on the wall and asked me who the woman was.

I said, 'That was my great-grandmother who came from Poland.' And she wanted to know how old she was in the photograph. And my beloved too wondered from what part of Poland she had come.

We stood around the picture, wondering about when Martha came to Dublin and why she was dressed in such a fancy costume and who had taken the picture. I couldn't answer a single question, yet there was something about Martha that insisted itself on me and was pushing its way up to the surface of our lives. Even just putting the photograph on the wall had somehow recovered a fragment of her. Her story was surfacing in the world, like a long-lost body floating to the surface of a lake.

Outside the window, there was something about the sloping fields, white with winter frost, and the rusting hay byre and willow trees withered on the ditch where our land touched our neighbour's fields that inclined me to the possibility that he too might not be entirely forgotten as long as we remembered his story and the small things he left in his wake.

All I remember of my father is a shadow under the standard lamp in a soft armchair with his wireless beside him, listening to BBC Radio 4, his books behind him, contained in a bookcase that Prospero might have envied.

He sat for years beneath that lamp, reading his newspapers as if they were maps and he was a ship's captain sailing on a lonesome ocean. Where he came from I never knew.

I kissed him formally every night before going to bed. His cheeks like hard sandpaper on my soft, downy face, his big lips on my forehead. It was as if he lived alone inside himself and had a mask to meet not just people on the street but even his wife and children as well. An isolation that kept my mother out and distanced her even from his bed at times, so that all her life she was condemned to weep and sing alone, though she was a perfect hostess and dexterous in conversation when strangers came to the front door. He isolated himself and melted into a shadow.

In 1976, he waited for death, smiling at the ceiling in the county home, whispering something about angels and drinking tea his wife had brought in a flask. And I saw tenderness in him as he was dying. I saw the vulnerability that comes when failing health opens the human heart, and he created a space in which she could be close to him at last and in which he could accept both love and death with equanimity.

'You're very good,' he said as he patted her on the head, and she left the room for a moment to wash the empty mug in the kitchen. When she returned he was gone.

My father was born in poverty and reared by his

grandmother. He was an oddball with no relations, no past or photographs or mementos. He disliked clergymen and never sat with us at Sunday Mass because, he claimed, the crowds made him dizzy, and so he remained alone in the back pew.

He became an accountant after years of struggle and night school and study, and was terrified of anyone knowing the details of his humble beginnings. Cavan in the 1950s was not a socially mobile world.

So no one questioned him as he sat for years under the light of the standard lamp in the front room, reading Chardin and Ezra Pound, H.G. Wells, G.K. Chesterton and Thomas Merton, Ethel Mannin and biographies and memoirs about people who had converted to Catholicism.

When I went into the room and sat on the sofa, I sometimes asked him about the woman who had reared him.

It seemed like she still lived in his heart. Sometimes, she seemed to be the only thing in his heart because the coldness with which he wrote a cheque each Friday at lunchtime at the dining-room table and passed it to my mother implied no emotion between them. It was a cheque for five punts, her weekly allowance for groceries.

His granny must have tended to him hand and foot, my mother would say because, even in old age, he prided himself on his inability to boil an egg. And in all those situations, eating his boiled eggs at the dining-room table,

264

or entertaining friends at parties in the golf club with recitations or doing imitations of Adolf Hitler or totting up the towers of little numbers in his ledger with a pencil behind his desk in the county council, he must have known about the medal. And if it had significance he must have known that too. A silver medal with an intricate pattern on the circle containing a Star of David and the ancient Hebrew letters that spelled out a blessing: Mazal.

Yet, he had it folded away with the receipts of a burial and a death certificate, for that woman he claimed he loved as a mother and who came from Poland.

He locked it all into his box of private documents, where it lay hidden for so many decades, after his death and my mother's death, until, by sheer accident or by design of the universe, it revealed itself to me.

'I'm going to Poland,' I said to the General one evening at the end of Christmas. It was 6 January, what in Ireland is called the Women's Christmas. The General always has a dinner, but he only invites men.

'The women are busy having their own fun,' he says. It's the only time in the year that he tolerates a dinner table of men.

The pudding was on the table when I told him.

'Wonderful. That's excellent. You're away from that woman of yours for too long. Absence is very dangerous in matters of love. You will have a holiday.'

'Not exactly.'

'What do you mean?'

'Well, I'm not going for a holiday. In fact, I'm not going to stay with her.'

'OK.'

'I'm just going to Poland.'

'Why?'

'Snow.'

'Snow?'

'Yes. I'm going for the snow. Like some people go skiing in the winter. Well, I don't ski. But I like the snow. It helps me write. That's why I went to Romania.'

'But that was a disaster,' he said. 'You got a perfect apartment, and just because they didn't put on the hot water immediately you had a tantrum and came running home with your tail between your legs.'

'Which is why I want to go again. I'm trying to overcome whatever fears I had last year,' I said. 'Whatever anxiety that blocked me from simply enjoying the beauty of Bucharest and all that snow. So now I want to go again.'

267

'To Romania?'

'No. Poland.'

'I'm confused,' he said.

But then I wasn't telling him the whole story.

On New Year's Eve, she had made the suggestion.

'Why don't you come to Warsaw, take a separate apartment and write. You'd love it. And we could meet in the evenings and have a great time.'

She knew that the isolation throughout the winter had damaged me. She knew I might not survive another six months at home without her. And as she was returning to work with the icon in the middle of January the sensible thing was for me to join her there.

'Have your own workspace and write,' she suggested. 'There could be snow.'

I couldn't find a reason to disagree.

I drove all the way from Leitrim to Dublin in the middle of the night on 18 January to be in time for the plane. I stopped at the Gala in Ballinaleck for a coffee. It's a vast floorspace of food for weary travellers. There are always dozens of cars coming and going, zooming in and out off the N7 in search of diesel, petrol, coffee, chips, burgers and other small sugary comforts.

I drank the coffee as I drove and at the airport I left the car in QuickPark and then jumped on the shuttle bus to Terminal One so fast that I forgot where I had left the car.

'Shit,' I hissed out loud on the bus and a lady opposite me looked from under her winter woollen hat with some disgust.

'My car,' I explained. 'I forgot where I left it.'

She held an expression of shock as if she had just swallowed an entire boiled egg, which suggested she wasn't tolerating any excuses for foul language from a strange hairy man.

The Dublin security personnel were loud, like turkeys in a small corral, and they maintained a constant noise as I took off my shoes, belt and disposed of everything in the trays.

'No liquids, please. Place your laptops in a separate tray, please. Over here, please. This way, please.'

Then I had breakfast and waited for the call to board flight FR5540.

I was in the front seat, 1C, and the traffic from the aisle behind me to the toilet beside the cockpit door constantly rubbed my leg, and the trolleys that the stewards shuttled up and down with coffee, tea, alcohol, perfumes and lottery cards forced me to wake from my dozing each time they needed to get by. Not that I was complaining. To lift into the air over North County Dublin was exhilarating. No matter how long the journey, no matter where the destination, I always feel excited. It had begun again. I was away.

The traffic to the toilet contained a smattering of young Polish women in high boots and tight jeans and figure-hugging jumpers, shirts and blouses, whose proximity was comforting as I headed across Europe in the hope of finding my great-grandmother.

From the Palace of Culture in midtown, I took the 171 to Rozbrat. My Airbnb apartment was on the fifth floor of a nineteenth-century building. It had three enormous windows and a balcony overlooking a hill of trees that were, on that particular evening, covered with snow.

Everything seemed to be as it had always been. There was an old creaking lift with three doors and a dark-wood interior. I imagined officers in Nazi uniforms standing beside me. In this old building, there must have been many moments when such people came and went, socialising with the inhabitants, listening to choral music by Vivaldi on the gramophone, eating sandwiches and drinking tea and whispering about the ghettos.

270

I livened up a packet of borscht soup with cloves of garlic and ate it with bread from a bakery on the street just outside the apartment block. I sat at the window in the dark, with my supper, gazing at the snow-covered hills and the trees.

The beloved called on Skype.

'So you arrived,' she said.

'Yes,' I said, 'and the flat is lovely. But a bit cold.'

'It's good that you're here,' she said.

'It was your idea,' I said.

'Is it snowing in Rozbrat?' she asked.

'Yes,' I replied. 'Is it snowing on Biela□ska?'

'Yes,' she said. 'It's wonderful.'

'It's beautiful,' I whispered.

We were talking like lovers already. We were talking with the same wonder we had years ago, staring out the bedroom window in the hills above Lough Allen when the child was in the cot and the sapling trees were merely twigs sticking up out of the winter snow.

'Are you working on your book tonight?' she asked.

'Yes,' I lied. 'I'm working. I've already begun.'

Because I didn't want to be swept up in her love too soon.

'So when will we meet?' she wondered.

'Well, I could write for a few days,' I suggested, 'and then we could meet at the weekend.'

She agreed that this was a good idea.

271

I couldn't sleep on the first night. The apartment overlooked a park. I looked out at the frosted trees like a white beard and the snow falling on the blue canopy of the skating rink like buds of cotton wool and the red-tiled roofs of other apartments in Rozbrat. I watched it all until the entire world had turned white. And then a full moon rose and flooded in through the long windows of the sitting room and the long window in my bedroom. I put on fleece leggings under my trousers and a double vest, shirt and jacket and wrapped a scarf around my face and with big boots I went out into the snow.

The animals and birds had gone to sleep. The humans were indoors and the streets were silent. I could see light in some windows, as if the people inside were waiting. Outside where I stood, it was still snowing.

In childhood, we were always waiting for something. We all waited as we sat around in pubs or near the open fire or in fields of summer. I used to think it was the essence of being Irish, to wait and doze by the fire. Waiting for friends, for letters, for the nine o clock news, for exam results, the visa in the post, the mother to die, the Mass to be over. There was a great patience in people back then. They waited.

But Ireland changed. We began to notice time. And everywhere we looked, it was slipping away and, eventually, we couldn't bear even to queue in a post office. We couldn't bear 'to waste time'.

But there is a deeper waiting, I thought, as I walked in the snow, making my way between the tall black trees, up the hill towards the statue of Charles de Gaulle, and then around by the Church of the Three Crosses, and back down through the woods again. I had come to Poland for nothing. I had no reason to be there. I had no cause to pursue or goal to attain in Warsaw. I was just waiting. Waiting for nothing.

I let go all my anxieties as I walked. I saw the details of my life like little specks of snow falling not into me but away from me. Dropping down into an endless pit below me, a deep white falling until I was just walking with no past or future.

I erased from my mind even this walking so that there was no me, apart from the sound of my feet like hushed hoofs in the snow and the sound of my breath and the colours of the city, the neon lights in the distance beyond the trees and on the tops of buildings as I walked through the whitened parkland.

When I returned to the apartment, I made some winter tea, with lemon, orange, apple, honey, cinnamon and a Barry's teabag. I switched on the little two-bar heater and relished the drink as I stared out at the still-falling snow.

I was exhausted. It was −7 outside and the cold assaulted my body because I was not used to such severity. Going outdoors was like stepping into an icy pool and, for an hour after my walk, I leaned over the heater and drank a steady flow of winter tea. My lungs were tight and heavy and I could hardly breathe. I feared I might have developed a chest infection.

The building in which I was living had survived the war. The wooden lift and shadowy corridors, with brown doors and old wrought-iron light fittings in the stairwell, had not changed much in sixty years. I imagined Nazi officers sitting where I sat, speaking about the wonders of Germany, homesick for Bavaria, all of them looking out the same window and gazing towards the same trees on the hill, beyond which, far away on the other side of the city, was the Jewish ghetto.

Snow fell most nights as I worked alone on this manuscript. Or at least that's what I said each time the beloved phoned. But I wasn't writing many sentences.

On the streets at night, women wore squeaky white anoraks and elaborate fur hats and stared out from behind scarves that masked their faces and protected their lungs from the cold air. All I could think of was Tolstoy.

My father always advised me to keep my chest warm. It was a rare fragment of intimacy from an otherwise aloof patriarch.

In fact, I don't think there was a day in Warsaw that I didn't wear thermal leggings. And I kept a scarf across my mouth, even on the bus and in the church on Nowy Świat.

I sometimes went for coffee across the road from the church before heading for prayer. One day, I forgot I had the scarf still across my mouth as I raised the cup to drink. I slobbered all over myself and cursed out loud and the young students shifted uneasily in their seats all around me.

It's not that I actually prayed in the church but the sound of the choir was delicious.

After a week of walking the cold streets and hugging the heater and drinking winter tea, my chest infection was bad enough to warrant attention. I went to a health clinic one afternoon and paid forty euro for a lady doctor to give me an ECG and then examine my lungs and prescribe ten days of antibiotics. I accepted it cheerfully and went back again to the apartment, where I spent the rest of that night sucking lemons, drinking vitamin C and watching the lights come on in the apartment block opposite me.

Watching the lights was comforting. It reminded me of the old days in west Cavan when I would sometimes stand at the door and admire the glowing windows in other houses scattered across the mountain and know that I was not alone.

The apartments in Warsaw had the same effect. Their lights came on in twos and threes, randomly, as folks returned home for the evening. I thought of each apartment in the block like a cottage and each block like a small village.

The old man downstairs, who had a mat outside his door for wiping his feet and a little blanket for his cat, came to me one night. Usually, the cat would wait on the street outside until someone was emerging from the hall door and then he'd slip in and up the concrete stairwell to the door where he waited patiently on the blanket for the old man to return home. The old man was stooped and whenever we met he was always carrying a small plastic shopping bag with milk, packets of instant soup and loaves of bread from the supermarket across the road on Bielańska Street.

I was lying in bed sucking lemons and feeling sorry for myself when there was a knock on the door. It was him. He looked distraught and I suspected he was saying something about the cat, but I couldn't understand and he had no English.

I kept saying, 'Sorry, sorry, I no speak Polish. Sorry.'

Eventually, this dawned on him and he turned his stooped body towards the stairwell and walked away, down into the darkness.

I lay in the bed for a while, thinking about him, and though I knew there was no God to intervene in the small calamities of our mediocre existence and make all things well, I was such an irrational animal that I did find myself overcome by an urge to pray that no harm might have come to his cat.

I walked every night, retracing my steps in the snow from the night before and watching the moon pallid above the blackened trees, then I'd go back to my apartment. The old me would have wanted to ask why. What was the meaning of me being in Warsaw? What was the point of walking every night? What was the reason to remain distant from the beloved? But the new me wanted to know nothing.

Just to walk was enough.

One night, I saw on a weather website that there was more snow farther west, near Łódź. I was still almost afraid to approach the beloved. Her embrace would quieten me. It would bring an end to my isolation. It would give me meaning at a moment when I wanted nothing. And I didn't want to be embraced or end my isolation just yet.

So I phoned her and said I was going to Łódź.

'Oh,' she said, 'I was looking forward to us getting together for the weekend. I thought you'd be finished work.'

'No, I won't. I might go on Friday evening to see Łódź. It's such an interesting city.'

'Do you want me to go with you?'

'No. I'll be trying to research. And maybe writing a lot. But next week I'll be finished. I'll be free. After I've been to Łódź.'

I had no reason to go to Łódź apart from the fact that I was still absorbed in a kind of dream. I was trying to touch something that can only be found in dreamtime or complete solitude. 279

The following day, Friday, I went on a train, just to walk around the old Jewish ghetto there in the snow and to watch the moon rise on a Friday evening and to realise that nothing much on the moon has changed and nothing much on earth.

The Grand Hotel on Piotrkowska Street is a world of old carpets, art deco, high ceilings and the hush of musty grandeur that has remained unchanged since 1900; a hotel that had kept the hot water running and the doors open continuously since then, though I didn't notice any other guests and, in the dining room, the waiter spoke in whispers.

I saw the moon again, pallid and waning above the blackened buildings that remain in the Łódź ghetto. As a Christian, I felt unease as I passed the red-bricked church near where the ghetto used to be. I felt a lump of shame in my chest and found it hard not to judge myself badly. Yet I had felt like a pilgrim on the train as it ploughed through windy snow towards Łódź on the eve of the Sabbath, and I felt like a pilgrim again as I walked the derelict streets that were once a hill of skulls.

Back at the hotel, I had a hot bath.

Afterwards, I watched from my window as men on a cherry picker cleared ice from the roof. Then I downloaded images of the moon and the sour, dark alleyways and backstreets that I had taken with my iPhone: young boys with earrings selling onions from the back of a white van and an old man pulling two bags of coal on a buggy as his wife lit a cigarette and held it to his lips in the freezing fog. And a hatless woman who dropped her bag of McDonald's burgers in the snow. I could smell the chips as she sighed and I wanted to hug her, to say I know how it feels to lose something. But neither she nor I knew what it might be like to lose everything. Yet.

Neither of us were Jews. At least it's not likely that she was part of whatever remained of the two hundred thousand who had lived in Łódź seventy years ago.

On the following day I went to a Jewish restaurant and devoured a bowl of chicken soup, but when I asked the girl who served me if the restaurant was owned by a Jewish family, she smiled sadly and said it wasn't.

I headed for the Teatr Wielki on Jaracza Street where

Madama Butterfly was playing. I stood on the steps outside the glass doors beside a scarcely human goose of a woman in middle age with a short neck who was smoking and staring at me. I stared back. Behind the glass, I saw another hundred women, all alarmingly identical beneath their furry hats, squashed together and chattering, as if they had just landed from the sky. They were crowded around the box office, so I abandoned any hope of getting a ticket and walked back to the hotel.

281

I returned to Warsaw on Sunday. From the train, I saw a man on the railway tracks in a yellow jacket chatting on his mobile. Perhaps he was talking to his wife about what to get in Tesco on his way home.

Heaps of snow were stacked up along the tracks and the salty falling of it, and the cloudy fog of it, and the very stillness in the middle of it – a whorl of whiteness where the railway worker disappeared and reappeared – made me wonder how close I was to the past when the trains were going east in 1943.

At the central station in Warsaw, the platform was frozen and crowded with young women in jeans so tight and boots so high that I thought I was back in Mullingar.

I couldn't open the carriage door. It was jammed – until an elderly woman snapped it open with one flick of her wrist. A slim orchid of a lady in fur. I held the door for her and passed her a suitcase before I too stepped onto the platform. We chatted briefly as she arranged her furs. Then she ungloved her hand and offered it to me.

'You are very kind,' she said.

When I woke the following morning, the antibiotics had clearly done their job, the cold was gone, my chest felt normal and clear and I knew it was time to visit the museum.

282 As I headed up through the old ghetto, there was a sad little Christmas tree lying on the street, a withered skeleton of someone's happiness.

Farther up the same street, I bought a sandwich of ham and cheese from a woman in a van at the corner of the roundabout. It cost me less than a euro but I couldn't eat it. The bread and cheese were stale and a soggy lettuce leaf sat in the middle of it, and then in the middle of the lettuce there was a human hair. I noticed it when I was trying to discard the lettuce. It was a long black hair, and it didn't come off my head. So I threw the entire sandwich in the bin and continued walking.

But, instantly, I was ashamed to think about what there might have been to eat in the ghetto on a sunny morning in January 1942 when the streets were white with snow.

Once Upon a Time

In the Polish Museum of Jewish History, I saw a sign for a resource centre where people could consult a researcher.

Magda was a slim woman with glasses and excellent English and she spoke with precision, like an academic.

'I am trying to find my great-grandmother.'

'OK,' she said, 'let's look for her.'

In a few moments, Martha Frith from Dublin became Morteh Frejd from Poland.

We went to a computer screen and we searched every region in Poland for such a name. We pressed the buttons. Clicked the mouse. Watched the screen filling up with data.

Within another few moments, Martha from Dublin who put her date of birth on the 1911 census as 1856 appeared on our screen as Morteh Frejd whose birth was registered in 1857.

We searched to see if Morteh did anything else in Poland, but we found no record. She did not marry or give birth or die. She vanished from Polish history. And, yes, I confirmed that Martha who was married in Ireland in 1876 had no story in Ireland before that date. On the Irish records, she was never born.

So we concluded that the woman in my photograph that my father had known as his only mother was the very same Morteh Frejd who had been born in Łóździeje, a small village six kilometres into Lithuania.

We concluded that the pogroms reported from the area of Suwałki in the decade when she vanished, including the burning of the wooden houses in which Jews had lived near the marketplace in that village, may have been the cause of her flight.

My father had said that she came to Ireland with her sister and, in the graveyard in Dundrum, there was a record to verify that, but it showed the so-called sister was twenty-five years older and perhaps, I thought, she came with her mother.

Would it not be likely that a mother and child might flee from burning buildings or from a husband who divorced them and married again? There could have been any number of reasons. Is it not possible that, like many other Jews in those decades, she may have made her way to a seaport, and a boat bound for London or Liverpool, and stayed there for a while, and then, as others did, drift across the sea to Dublin?

Maybe she took with her a medal, a silver pendant with

the Star of David on it, and the Hebrew word for blessings on it, just as a keepsake, as something with which to remember her childhood, her village before she left – and maybe she clung to that medal as her lucky charm, through the days of love and children and poverty until her death in a cottage on Beaver Row in Donnybrook, Dublin, in 1932.

How can I ever know how it passed to her grandson, my father? Did she tell him her story and gather for him in that medal all the soft and beautiful memories of her life as a child in Poland, to let him know that she had loved it there? Did she speak Polish or Yiddish back then? Did religion mean as much as a hen's tooth to her? I don't know. All I know is that she ventured out and found new worlds, and loved and died and was buried in Dundrum, her bones perhaps with her mother's bones, all wrapped up together in the silence of the grave.

Whether she did or did not tell my father any of these things I can never know. Because her story ended with him. With my father's silence, through all those years in the drawing room under the light of a standard lamp, that for some reason I detested as an object in the world.

I can never find the real Martha, though I held a photocopy of what may have been her birth certificate in my hand and saw the scrawl of some official's hand spelling out her name and her father's name. But I could never fill in the years she lived on earth, no matter how wonderful or beautiful or tragic they had been. She is gone. Gone so completely that I could not know if my Martha was even the same Martha that the researcher Magda had found in her files.

I thanked Magda and folded the birth cert in my pocket and walked out into the snow falling on the streets of Warsaw.

288

All I can do is imagine. Or fill in the story as a storyteller
does. Like this.

Once upon a time, in a far-off forest somewhere in a
quiet village, a child was born called Morteh Frejd, to a
mother who was called Anna or Enna and a father who
was Berko Rubinowitch. That's all I know. What happened
next is anybody's guess.

A grandfather takes down a pipe, perhaps, at evening
time and smokes it in the corner with quiet pleasure, the
day the child is born.

A mother wipes a tear from her eye, the day the girl first
sings a love song.

A girl says a prayer the night of her first dance. She
powders her face, puts scent in her hair. The biggest night
of her life. Stepping onto the dancefloor for the first time.

Is that how her story might have begun?

Was there one special boy among the dancers that she
longed to kiss?

Did the moon shine on the Star of David pendant as it lay beside her brushes and her perfumes? Did she pick it up and clasp it around her neck?

They ran away, perhaps. But who? Her mother and herself? Or were there others?

Nothing can be said with certainty. The routes through the forest. Through the cities. In fear of strangers and hard winters. Children of the wandering Aramaic. The plotline of a thousand movies.

Don't lose that medal.

290 Walking into a shop in Dublin where a young man was selling calico. Within a year, she had become his bride. Pembroke Road. A small house.

Don't lose that medal. Where did I leave it? Where did she get it?

From some uncle she left behind, perhaps? Someone caught in the fires? Or her grandfather?

'My dearest love,' she might have written, 'Thank you for the pendant. It is beautiful. I will cherish it all my life, and it will remind me of you.'

I make it up line by line. I see her feet crunch through the forest. Four buckets in her hands. I make it up.

The only chance she had of being remembered was my father. He might have said more, as he sat under his standard lamp for years and read books by Ethel Mannin, Thomas Merton, Pierre Teilhard de Chardin and Malcolm Muggeridge. He was an articulate man.

He said that when he fell one day in the school yard and an ink pen stabbed his hip, it was his grandmother Martha who came and carried him to hospital.

He said she cooked strange soups and her pots had lids. But the man under the standard lamp, who didn't like sitting with his family in church and who, when I went to a Catholic seminary, sent me cuttings from newspapers with advertisements for jobs in the civil service, never told me the full story.

It wasn't an accident that he kept her medal and the detailed receipts for her burial in his box of documents. When he had sat under the standard lamp he had known that they were there. Directly above him, in the bedroom where he slept. On a shelf in the wardrobe. I suppose he might have had his own fears. He might have known stories that he felt should never be told. He may have tried to bury everything and, in turn, he may have buried the most beautiful part of himself. Who knows?

They call it trans-generational trauma.

Because we sometimes carry the echoes of wounds that we never knew and atrocities that happened to others before we were born. Famines and burnings and rapes all swallowed, buried deep within our ancestors' psyches and then passed on to the following generations as pain without labels. Photographs without stories. But we need the labels nonetheless, as we need our ancestors, like lovers, demons or angels, to help us sometimes and straighten out the complex and knotted thread of our own existence.

My father had his secrets. Yet he could not resist the accountant's instinct to take care of the paperwork. The details. The receipts for the burial, and an old medal. Just enough to form the basis of a story.

He was her last possible chance on earth to have her story told.

'Take this,' she might have said, reaching out her old hand with the medal before she died.

'Why?' he might have asked.

'Because I liked it.'

Which is where it ended for her. Although I don't know if she said that. Because I don't know anything.

All around me in Warsaw, there were other stories. No
matter how bleak the world, there are strangers everywhere
who have lived lives of terrible intensity that need to be
spoken about. The moment I walked out onto the street,
into the world, there were accidents waiting to happen and
stories waiting to surface in every casual conversation.

Three years ago, I went to Warsaw for the first time and,
using an Airbnb apartment, I had written the first draft of
a book about my mother. I used to eat on the street at the
same place every day. It was a Lebanese restaurant, which
had a small kiosk serving takeaway falafel, and I usually
stopped there to have a chat with the boy from Bangladesh
who prepared the food.

He asked me where I was from.

'Leitrim,' I declared.

'Is that an independent country?' he wondered.

'It is part of Ireland but colonised by Dublin, London and Washington,' I explained. 'What remains of our own way of life – accordion music, pig farming and a flair for conversation – has been mostly extinguished by our masters.'

'Ah,' he said, 'I understand; so Leitrim is like Scotland.'

'Exactly,' I agreed, impressed by his clarity.

'I have seen Mel Gibson film,' he explained. '*Braveheart.*'

'Yes,' I agreed. 'Leitrim is like that. And *Vikings*. If you really want to know what life is like in Leitrim, watch *Vikings*.'

I bought a bottle of water and started munching the falafel as I stood on the street and he came outside the kiosk with a mug of tea and lit himself a cigarette. Both of us stared at the skyscrapers and I felt close to him, as exiles feel with others who are far from home. I raised my bottle of water and offered a toast to our two great nations – Leitrim and Bangladesh.

He said Bangladesh was a good country. 'Many fish in rivers and green countryside with fruit and vegetables, and beautiful trees.'

I felt he wanted me to like Bangladesh. I felt he wanted to believe that I wasn't wearing clothes that people are forced to make in sweat factories for the Western market. I felt he wanted to believe that a bit of Leitrim wasn't completely colonised by the great capitalist Satan that tears communities apart with its multinational claws.

'I'll see you again,' I promised as I left. Each time I returned, he smiled. 'How is Leitrim man this evening?'

'Good,' I would reply. 'And how is everyone in Bangladesh?'

'Everyone is good,' he would say.

Of course everyone in Bangladesh was not good. Everyone in Warsaw or Leitrim was not good.

But I often thought about him when I was back in Ireland, touring the country doing readings from that same book about my mother, which I had begun writing at that time.

At a certain hour of the evening when I was in some theatre in Longford, Sligo or Kerry, waiting to go out onto the stage and tell stories to strangers, I would think of him, leaning over his kiosk waiting for strangers to buy a falafel for ten zloty. He would be with me, like Jesus, in the mornings during summertime when I was in the garden in Arigna, and the breeze shook the dry leaves from the trees, and me thinking of Bangladesh as more than just a musical word but as another garden where trees grow and are cherished by other people who live there.

I planted acorns one autumn that fell from a tree that survived the war in Saski Park – and if they grow they will remind me of the boy from Bangladesh who made his living on the streets of Warsaw. I will keep him near me, even though when I returned to Warsaw in 2016 I went to the street where his shop had been and found it all boarded up, and there was no sign of him anywhere.

In fact, even when I drifted into the Polish Museum of Jewish History, I felt humbled to be on the margins of such an immense sea of stories, individual and collective, infinitely more significant than the one I had lost. Walking around the museum was like gazing into an ocean of catastrophe, bearing witness to that singularly most important event in modern European history, the *Shoah*. And all about me I could also sense smaller narratives surfacing: at the cloak desk, the ticket desk and in the cafeteria, or in the dark corners of various exhibit rooms where elderly people discreetly wiped tears from their eyes and old withered and gnarled hands held each other in joy and pride.

While I was sitting in the museum restaurant, a woman from America approached me and asked if I had the password for the internet. She was frail but ferocious as she glared out through enormous spectacles. I said I didn't because I was using my own internet connection.

'I didn't know you could do that,' she said, as if my internet capability might imply a suicide bomb in my vest.

But she had already sat down beside me with her MacBook nestled in a goofy big leather handbag.

'Where the hell is my coffee?' she wondered.

296

She was holding a little plastic marker with the number five on it.

'I'm waiting ten minutes for my coffee,' she explained, 'and they still haven't brought it.'

She fiddled with the number five in her hand.

'I think I'll just go up and ask that guy,' she said, focusing on a waiter in a white shirt who was passing by with a tray of cakes.

'Excuse me,' she said, 'I ordered a coffee, and it hasn't come.'

'It's OK,' he said, smiling. 'We know about you. Your coffee is coming soon.'

Then he walked away.

'He knows about me?' she said. 'You hear that? What does that mean?'

'This is a beautiful museum,' I said, 'but working in a restaurant is not easy. In fact,' I added, 'I know a woman here in Warsaw who works in an Asian restaurant twelve hours a day and never gets to sit down.'

'That's terrible,' the American said. 'Is she Chinese?'

'I don't think so,' I said, knowing that there are more nationalities in Asia than just Chinese.

'Chinese people can stand longer. They weigh less. Is she a friend of yours?'

'No,' I said. 'I just happen to go there for the food.'

'Oh, I thought you knew her,' she said.

Her coffee arrived.

'So what are you doing here?' she asked. 'Are you a tourist?'

I was getting alarmed at the directness of her questions.

I said, 'Actually, I'm looking for my great-grandmother.'

'Your great-grandmother,' she repeated incredulously. 'Is she in a wheelchair?'

'No,' I said, 'she died almost one hundred years ago. I'm just doing some research on the family tree. And you?' I added, presuming she was at the same game.

'I just saw the building and came in to use the bathroom,' she declared, 'and have a coffee. Warsaw is damned cold.'

298

I was in another restaurant one afternoon, sitting at a small table by the window with an American-style menu where all the foods were displayed in images: juicy burgers with forests of lettuce on top.

The yellow trams outside had their lights on and the blue light of an ambulance was flashing at the entrance to a building across the street. I was excited because I was meeting the beloved later in the day. It was our first meeting since I'd left Ireland.

A mother and daughter sat at the table next to me. The teenager wore a white-wool knit jumper and high black boots. She had blonde hair and wiped her mouth very delicately with a serviette every time she placed a morsel of potato between her lips. The older woman watched her like a mother swan.

'Are you here on business?' the waiter asked.

'Yes,' I said, 'I have a very important meeting this afternoon. With my beloved.'

The waiter wasn't going to venture further into what he thought might be a minefield.

'Ah yes,' he said, as he placed a credit card machine on the table beside me. 'You like to pay in euros or zlotys?'

'Euros,' I replied.

'Of course,' he said, 'you are Irish.'

'How do you know?' I wondered.

'I watch *Father Ted* continuously,' he replied, without the slightest irony.

299

The swans at the next table watched me put on my coat with the clarity of animals who are feeding and detect a beast from elsewhere close by.

I left the restaurant and strolled through the crowds towards Old Town and into a small bar where the beloved and her teacher were waiting for me. She was full of excitement. We embraced.

'How did Łódź go?' she asked.

'Like a dream,' I replied.

'And the Polish Museum of Jewish History?'

'Yes. I found her,' I declared. 'I found her. Or at least I think I did.'

The icon maker was listening all the time, sitting on a high stool, nursing a whiskey and waiting to be introduced.

Andrei was a small man of middle age from Belarus who wore old shirts and drank whiskey with a quiet passion. We shook hands and all three of us settled on high stools in the bar. Andrei had worked across Europe for years. He spent a decade in Berlin with elite auction houses, restoring paintings and period furniture, but his passion was the icon. He had written them as large as life on the walls of churches from Moscow to Minsk. In Smolensk, he worked on a great façade for the cathedral there, creating a mosaic seven metres high just below the dome and using over one million tiny mosaic pieces, twenty-seven thousand of them in gold.

His eyes devoured me, as if he was terrified or hungry or was wondering what nature of flesh I had before he might eat me.

I began fiddling with my phone, found Spotify and tapped 'Russian Choir' so that the little snug of tiny white lights filled with the chanting of Orthodox monks. The lady behind the bar wagged her finger in disapproval, but the icon maker was delighted.

'When I am working on an icon, I listen to the monks all day with my earphones,' he said. 'The music helps me physically.'

He made a gesture with his elbows, holding them out like wings.

'The music holds my arms up,' he said, 'so I don't get tired.'

There were large crowds heading into the church across the street.

301

'God,' I said, pointing out the window. He laughed, as if he understood this to be a word that has outlived its meaning for many Western Europeans.

Yet as we drank more whiskey, I wanted to tell him that I felt lonely without God. I wanted to tell him that beyond the loneliness of being separated from my beloved, or losing neighbours, beyond the loneliness of grief after death, there is nothing more cutting than the blade of awakening that opens the heart when the last fragrance of God has dissolved.

And because it's easy to move from the winter lights in a Warsaw bar to a feed of spinach dumplings, we finished our whiskeys and went to a low, caverned cellar where a collective matriarchy sat like fat cats at their soup.

Andrei was an angel, as clear as the presence that long ago had tiptoed down the stairs and touched my shoulder when I was a child sitting on the bottom step playing with the figures in the Christmas crib. There was some stillness in his gaze that pinned me down. I imagined him on the outside wall of the cathedral in Smolensk, on the scaffolding, with his little golden bricks and his eyes fixed on the image. We ordered goulash and bread and Russian pierogi, and we ate almost everything in silence.

'What do you think?' the beloved asked me when Andrei had slipped away for a moment to the bathroom.

'I think he's amazing,' I said.

302 'I can't find my brother,' he said eventually, when the food was finished, as he stared across the table at us, because he also held in his heart a universe of stories that I had only begun to open.

I dined with him again the following evening in a beer hall beside the university, where he offered his stories in broken English over a plate of pierogi as we sipped beer, and gradually I put together how he became a maker of icons.

'I was four years old,' he said, 'when the icons appeared. My father and mother went for a walk one day, and I was in the house on my own. So I decided to draw. I saw very clearly there were white walls all around me so I thought nobody can see me. I will use the wall to draw.'

And so he did. When his father and mother returned

they went up to the wall and examined his drawings but they said nothing to chastise him because the drawings were imitations of images he would have seen in church.

'The next morning I get out of bed,' he said, 'and I see that my father and mother have worked all night to make the wall white. And I see that my drawings had disappeared and the white wall had reappeared.'

When his parents went to work, the child began all over again. But, this time, he used a chair so he could make more drawings on the wall.

'The next day the white wall came back again and so I thought my mother and father were preparing the wall for me every night.'

One day, a friend of his father's went up close to the wall and, for two minutes, he said nothing. Then he said to the father, 'I think you must show these images to somebody important.'

So a famous artist was invited to the house and he asked the child to draw something, and, after two hours, another naive icon appeared on the wall, and the artist said, 'You must leave this child with me. And he must begin work.'

That's the way some people understand icons. They appear. When you realise that they appear, then your life changes. Everything that you thought was real becomes imbued with possibilities of transcendence.

'When you bring an icon into the house, it changes your life,' he said. 'Eventually, it will change your family and

303

every one that belongs to you. It will change the neighbours who live close to you,' he said.

'And how can that be?' I wondered.

He glanced at the ceiling and blew through his teeth. There was nothing more that could be said. And there were things in my heart I knew would not survive if I tried to articulate them in the simple English that both of us were clinging to in order to communicate.

304   I don't use the word 'soul' anymore, at least not in public. But I suppose it's a word that troubled me at that time. I worried about it. For the previous two years, I'd had a sense that my soul was sour or rotting. My core, that which cannot be examined or its existence proven but which leads me through the forest, had begun to decay. The hidden architect of all my actions, the wise man at the back of the cave, had gone blind.

Which is why I had started putting bird boxes on the trees the previous summer. It wasn't to lure tits into domestic bliss. It was to entice the ghosts of previous lives to inhabit the woods again and to reawaken in me that thing called soul.

It sounds crazy in a secular world. Soul is a thing not spoken of nowadays. In time, everything withers, but still I cling to it – my soul, my inner self – and it is unpleasant to think that it might have gone sour.

Because without soul, I am only a monster. I see a person with my face, brushing teeth as he grins in the mirror, but I know he is a sham, a fake and an empty shell. I am afraid to go inside him, to visit his unspeakable dark, to make raids on the land below his silence for fear that I might find something rotten. I cling to the surface and complain about the government or generally share the collective unease that vibrates from radios, televisions and computer screens.

Once upon a time, seven years ago, I had an argument about the dishwasher and I went in search of the modern world and I left all my trees behind me in Leitrim. It was a mistake, because the trees had been a kind of sanctuary for my soul. Not that I could have taken them with me on the back of a truck since I was heading off to live in an urban apartment. But when I finally returned, I couldn't bear to go into the garden. I felt guilty because I had planted those trees as young saplings and then I had abandoned them. They had grown tall without me and I was alienated from them.

I thought of the trees every morning as I walked in Saski Park, at a little distance from the traffic, with other people: elderly couples entwined at the elbows, single men with their dogs or young couples absorbed with the contents of their buggies. I would sit at the water fountain, beneath the trees, and watch Warsaw wake up. One morning, I saw a wedding couple sitting up on the back of a bench like teenagers do, with big anoraks hiding his tuxedo and her long white wedding dress. They were kissing, their woollen hats touching. They seemed relaxed, as if they had already been to church and were relishing the feel of the world made new by their commitment to each other. I passed them as unremarkable as a ghost.

Yet I spoke nothing of how I felt to the beloved. Perhaps
because there is an appropriate time for intimacy and
an appropriate time for solitude. And my solitude had
changed in her absence. It was no longer frightening or
darkly lit, but more like a cloud where a bird soars and
wings the wind and is delightfully alone. And there is a
dignity in solitude that is sustained by a good relationship.
There are rooms where a person needs to go alone. And can
never speak of them. Never name them. The damage that
religion does when it is misused is to destroy the dignity of
that private space. It can do to the soul what pornography
does to the body.

So I walked around Warsaw with her, linked arms with
her and laughed mildly and listened attentively as she
spoke.

We went about with people in a polite way and we both
knew that the winter had been one of those times when a

partner becomes the custodian, the guardian, the sentry at the remote boundary of an unknown territory called the beloved.

We walked around the city of Warsaw, shopping, eating, drinking in bars and restaurants – like the old days in Dublin. And over us all the time was the shadow of Andrei, the icon maker, who told me stories that were like maps of the human psyche, and sometimes he would say, you must never tell this story to anyone – and I never did.

308

The beloved had made other friends in Warsaw, and one evening I accompanied her on a visit to a couple who lived on the top floor of an apartment block where it was impossible to see the walls because of all the paintings, books and African masks that clutter the four tiny rooms and the gigantic plants that grew from tiny pots on the long window ledge.

I called them the Squirrels because they never threw anything out. The souvenirs of a lifetime were stacked up to the ceilings of wood that sloped towards large windows where they both sat and observed the lights coming on in the apartments of the block opposite them.

We were eating at a round table on which an image of the Polish pope and a few holy pictures were propped against a television set that was never turned off. Mrs Squirrel worked in the library and she was a devout Catholic.

Mr Squirrel told me that he was delighted with the new government. He assured me that they would get things done.

'They are putting many things in order,' he explained. 'It was long overdue.'

There was an uneasy pause in which I made no comment.

Eventually, he asked me what I was writing about in Poland.

'It's hard to say,' I replied. Which was true. And after all we were their dinner guests, and I didn't want to be too grim in the face of Mrs Squirrel's renowned religiosity.

There were blurred images of the American primary election in Iowa coming through on the television screen that caught our attention.

'Who is Trump?' Mrs Squirrel wanted to know as she gazed at his strange head.

'He wants to be the president of America,' Mr Squirrel said. She raised her eyebrows as if the very look of Donald Trump made that idea ridiculous.

But since we were on the subject of politics, I mentioned the refugees in Europe and Mr Squirrel said it was certain that 'these people will come in and either take our jobs or do no work and be dependent on the state. There is no good outcome,' he explained, 'if you allow strangers into your home.'

Then he bent over his beloved and asked her if she

309

would like coffee and she said yes, as if he had never asked the question before.

While he was away, she directed me to the little sofa just a metre away from the table.

'Shall we sit over here?' she asked, as if I was Chopin and this was a palace long ago.

'Do you know Mr Putin?' she asked me, still gazing at the television screen.

'Not personally,' I said.

'He frightens me,' she whispered, and it felt like she was talking about someone who lived in the apartment below them.

From where we were sitting on the sofa, I could see the street still festooned with Christmas lights and elaborate street decorations.

I told her I had been to the Church of the Three Crosses and it was lovely to see the Christmas trees on either side of the altar, with fairy lights in the branches, and the crib at the side still there at the end of January, full of wise men and sheep.

The Squirrels are in their sixties and their body language is slow and devout, reflecting the ease of a couple who have transcended the wounds of a life-long marriage. They stole little intimate glances at each other when they thought I was not looking.

Earlier, they had explained to me that in the old days, when they were growing up, they had always looked to

Russia. They spoke the language and were engaged with the politics and on several occasions had taken a train to St Petersburg.

'But not anymore,' Mrs Squirrel said, as she glanced at Pope John Paul II behind the television set.

'But I have many brochures,' Mr Squirrel said, 'for the ballet.' And he got up and began fingering through a pile of old LP record sleeves stacked in the corner.

'Now, now,' Mrs Squirrel said, 'I think we are forgetting something,' as she stared at the empty cups and the tall pot of coffee on the table.

He abandoned his search for the brochures instantly.

'Ah, the milk!' he exclaimed, laughing and touching the top of her head affectionately as he passed. 'Yes, of course, I forgot the milk again.'

The manner in which his fingers stroked her hair and his lips touched the crown of her head had in it all the devotion of a monk's lips on the surface of an icon.

Everyone spoke. The Squirrels and the icon maker and the American woman in the museum. There was no end to it. We told Andrei about our life together, and he told us how his father had died, and it was as if we all needed to tell our stories just to know we existed.

When we had reached that fluidity – speaking and telling and sharing our stories – gradually we needed fewer words. The stories tapered off, and we were led out beyond the words, until, eventually, we passed hours in bars and on the streets and in the back pew of the Church of the Three Crosses in complete silence.

Which is how my visit ended. Me and her and him in silence. And then hugs. And then me on the plane alone. On my way home in silence. Not so much in solitude then. More embraced perhaps. By her. By him. By the woman at the boarding gate. By the air steward. By the passengers. By the world. Embraced. Entangled. That was the feeling. That was good.

The Time of Swallows

In the summer of 2012, when my mother died and my religious faith was still intact but crumbling, or about to crumble, a strange new discovery fell into my lap.

I attended a summer school in Donegal for no particular reason that I could put my finger on at the time. It was an Irish-language summer school. My teacher was from Belfast. He had a PhD in grammar, and he spoke about the genitive case with the singular passion of a warrior in the new Islamic state examining the hem of a woman's dress.

I was tired after the drive home from Gweedore and there was no one in the house at noon. She must have gone to Carrick-on-Shannon, I guessed, to shop. So I went to bed and slept for a few hours. Later, when she came in the back door, I heard her in the kitchen.

It was still the time of the buttercup. The time of the dandelion had not yet arrived. The time of the finches plundering the white fur spores of the opened spear thistles had not yet come but the meadow pipits were tweeting furiously in the neighbour's field, and a lone curlew was warbling somewhere in the heavens. The seedy days of July were still ahead of us. I went into the kitchen and saw two mugs of tea on the table. I picked one up and went into the sun room. I was looking out the window at the mountain, which was covered with the warm intense light of the slanting evening sun, when she came in with her mug. The heather was blazing. I was considering the name of the mountain.

316 'Sliabh an Iarainn,' I said, 'means the mountain of iron.'

It was the time of the swallows. Their first clutches were out of the nests and I was watching their low-flying antics as they swam though the still air and picked their dinner up close to the earth. The evening sun drew us out onto the patio. With binoculars, I followed a magpie wiping his beak, sensing the ground, pulling a slug up and devouring it. We were sitting shoulder to shoulder, like old people watching a cricket match.

'What are you thinking?' she asked.

'Sliabh an Iarainn,' I repeated. 'Did you know that Sliabh an Iarainn is the genitive case?' I said.

It's something I had not considered before.

'It's good to know you learned something on the Irish course.'

'Yes,' I replied.

When we had finished the tea, she took my cup and went

inside. I was still thinking about the mountain, and the Irish language, and the ex-priest I had met on the course, but I didn't mention any of that to her. It doesn't matter what you're thinking of after a few years. In the long unfolding of a relationship, it becomes less important. The fascination that burned on lovers' pillows when we were young and wet from sex had gone. In those days every little thing she said seemed amazing, and she listened to me with great intensity.

But that time was long gone. It's not that she knows what I am thinking now, but she knows that whatever is in my head is of no significance.

By accident, I had learned something in Donegal. Something more than the genitive case use for a mountain's name. I had discovered a language of love. Not a new language, but a way of using the language I already had.

It happened like this.

One day, I was sitting at the back of the classroom with a grammar book on the desk when a new student slipped into the seat beside me. A strong-featured man with hair turning grey and the curiosity of an eagle.

'A Mhichíl,' he said, 'is it yourself, by God?'

(That's just a translation.)

'It is me surely, by God,' I replied.

We didn't speak in English so our conversation was limited. At the coffee break, we shared a plate of gingernut biscuits and chatted about the upcoming Armagh–Donegal match.

'Is it yourself will be looking at the match?' I wondered.

'No,' he replied, 'I am not looking at it. But perhaps I might be in it.'

That sounded like he was on the team, and I could see why Armagh was the underdog if they were fielding players in their mid-fifties. But then he corrected his grammar.

'Accept my apology,' he said. 'Accept my thousand sorrows. What is being said with me is that I am going to the game. I will be looking at the match from the stage.'

He meant the stand, but we had so few words.

318 'That's amazing,' I said. Again because I didn't have the words to say 'that's interesting'.

And thus we talked our pidgin Irish each morning, like shell-shocked veterans of our long lives and our own private catastrophes, because we were stuck with the limited phrases of our college days when we were both studying for the priesthood. Of course, we might have had a lot to talk about if we were fluent in Irish or if we were speaking in English. He'd left before ordination, and I'd stayed in for a few short years, knowing that, in the end, there was no place in the Church for me.

We might have spoken of the extraordinary journey into decline that the Church had made in our time. We might have cross-referenced other clerics. Played the game of 'Where are they now?'

The liberals who went morose but stayed in the clergy because they felt it was too late to go. They thought they were old when they were forty. The ones in denial about sex abuse who just grew angry and bitter and blamed journalists for causing the Church's decline and for having no compassion for clerics. And the lonely ones who were burdened by their unlived gay lives, the ones who longed for the touch of a lover and who ended up teaching boys in grim Victorian secondary schools and getting ill and keeping bottles of whiskey in the wardrobe. And the naive ones who always kept saying that things would be different in the future. Some new pope would make a difference, they hoped.

But nobody did make a difference.

Finally, young new ones arrived, as if straight out of their mother's wombs and already in uniform and ordained, with smooth cheeks and zeal for the one true religion and almost completely ignorant of anything else. There was a lot we could have spoken of, if we'd been speaking English or if we'd been fluent in the native Irish tongue. We could have gossiped a bit and expressed shock at the state of the world. Or we might just have spoken of the women in our own lives, and how they had shifted our perspective over the years and of how naive we had been back then.

But we discussed none of these things. Because we didn't have the vocabulary. Our simple phrases claimed nothing. Said nothing. Engaged in no complex ideas. Everything was kept simple and, eventually, we pared the entire cosmos down to very simple phrases.

'The day is good.'

'The day is bad.'

'The day is amazing.'

(*Lá maith. Droch lá. Lá iontach.*)

When it rained he said, 'Today, it is raining.'

And when it was overcast, I really impressed him by declaring, 'It is cloudy today, and there will probably be a strength of rain by lunchtime.' That was a long speech in the linguistically restricted world in which we were conversing.

'You have the truth there,' he replied, admiring my fluency. Little did he know how devoted I am to the weather forecast on TG4.

Some days, I longed for a more complex conversation. I wanted to know how he had fared in the world over the decades and I wanted to talk to him about ageing and depression and all the other anxieties of modern life. But it couldn't happen. We were forced to discipline our tongues and find pathways towards each other in simple sentences. We couldn't get personal, in the way old friends usually do, by gossiping about the past. Instead, we relied on the landscape for small talk and we tried to avoid the future tense, the continuous past and the notorious conditional tense simply because we didn't have the verbs at our fingertips. Instead, we held to the exquisite condition of being in the present moment.

'Are you good today?'

'Yes, today I am good.'

And eventually, like a haiku, the changing sky became a metaphor for how we felt, and the weather outside the window carried our emotions. We narrowed ourselves into small phrases. We bent the empirical world to our own capacity for expression.

'Lá brea' began to mean everything.

We had fallen by accident into a state of zen. We were alive and human, sitting in each moment like magpies on an ash tree.

When the course was over, I packed my bag and cleared out of the house in Rannafast where I had been staying. I packed my notebooks and a book about Tory Island and the grammar book the teacher had been referring us to all week. But I knew I would never use them again. Flipping through the pages of the grammar, *Cruinnscríobh na Gaeilge*, felt like a lost life. All those verbs and nouns and other beautiful words would never be mine. It was too late. The Gaelic language I had tried to learn as a child was gone from me forever. But the week had taught me that through simple sentences, the mind can remain very much in the present moment. Instead of being uneasy that the beloved and I sometimes said very little to each other over the dinner table, I realised that we had, over the years, been practising the language of love.

So there we were on the patio, looking at the mountain

when I mentioned it's name. Sliabh an Iarainn, Mountain of Iron; the genitive case.

She wanted to know what a genitive case was. I told her I didn't know. And then she was gone. And then she was back. It happens like that. We have conversations with a few sparse words. But sometimes we move in and out of the room three or four times in the same sentence.

'That's a lovely evening,' she said, returning to the patio door.

And I said, 'Yes. It is.'

322

In the summer of 2016, my beloved returned from Poland.
I picked her up at the airport and we drove out to Dún
Laoghaire to visit friends and then, before midnight, we
headed for Leitrim. She had completed her work on the
icon. She didn't know if she might return to Poland. I
suspected that in view of how enriching she had found it,
she might be very likely to return again sometime in the
future.

But for a little while still, we would be together in the hills
above Lough Allen, another summer of uncertain weather
and dandelions, weeds, buttercups, horseflies, bees, flowers
and fruitful trees.

As she was unpacking she said, 'I have something for
you.'

I had not been expecting a gift, but I watched her unzip
the bag and open up the parcel and unravel the white gauze
and the bubble wrap to expose the *Icon of Kazan*.

'I thought you were doing it for the museum,' I said.

'I did one for the museum,' she said. 'Which remains in the museum. But I did another one. This one is for you. It's a gift.'

It was crafted perfectly in the likeness of the great Theotokos of Kazan housed in the National Museum in Warsaw which I had seen in photographs. The richness of the gold, the texture of the mineral painting, the still and compassionate gaze of the Mother reminded me of the stillness in the *Mona Lisa*.

324 Early the following morning, I cleaned the old bookcase belonging to my father. I took out all the shelves but one and lined it with blue silk scarves from the Buddhist Centre in Bawnboy and I placed the icon at the centre on the shelf.

Then I stood for a moment, gazing at it. The morning light was picking up the gold in the halo around Her face. The face was still in shadow, but it grew more deep in its expression as the light increased.

It has been a long road, I thought. Absorbing the waves of faith that move through me over the years and feeling the loss of it when the waves ebb and a low tide of anxiety reveals in me the dregs of a swamp.

Now, again, the circle was complete. It's not that I had recovered any religious belief. But I was still standing. And standing now before the icon.

Then I placed it on the shelf and closed the bookcase doors so that it was hidden from view. I turned the key in the lock. The icon was safe, behind the glass and the layers of silk that hung inside the bookcase doors. She had given me something precious. A gift I had not expected.

Nor had I expected my hands to shake so much as I turned the key in the lock.

I walked outside and found her. She happened to be sitting again looking at Sliabh an Iarainn across the lake. I joined her at a wrought-iron table on the new patio. And behind us were the glass doors into the extension, the new bedroom, a goldfish bowl of light, with a mighty oak bed big enough for both of us.

We were looking at the mountain in the distance, beyond the wide waters of Lough Allen. To our side, were the oaks and beeches, the willows and alders puffed out with luminous green leaf. Although in the sloping fields around us there were no cattle, no black beasts with warm furry heads reaching their snouts across the fence to be touched by a human hand. Because our neighbour's hand would touch no more, and his feet would move no more across the fields. He was at rest in the cemetery on the far side of Arigna Valley. And if the beloved was thinking about him at that moment, she did not say. Nor did I speak. Because there is a time for everything. A time for stories. And a time for silence.

Acknowledgements

With thanks to Ciara Doorley, Marianne Gunn O'Connor, Róisín Ingle, Brenda Doherty, Sophia Harding, Brendan Harding, Patrick McManus and the Venerable Panchen Ötrul Rinpoche.

And, as always, thanks to Cathy Carman – artist, collaborator and life-long companion.

And not forgetting Charlie and Miss Peabody, the warrior cats who accompanied me on this journey.

STARING AT LAKES

Throughout his life, Michael Harding has lived with a sense of emptiness – through faith, marriage, fatherhood and his career as a writer, a pervading sense of darkness and unease remained. When he was fifty-eight, he became physically ill and found himself in the grip of a deep melancholy. Here, in this beautifully written memoir, he talks with openness and honesty about his journey, and how, ultimately, he found a way out of the dark, by accepting the fragility of love and the importance of now.

Staring at Lakes started out as a book about depression. And then became a story about growing old, the essence of love and marriage - and sitting in cars, staring at lakes.

THE NUMBER ONE BESTSELLER
'WONDERFUL' *THE IRISH TIMES*

Hanging
with the
Elephant

A STORY OF
LOVE, LOSS AND
MEDITATION

MICHAEL HARDING

HANGING WITH THE ELEPHANT

Left alone in his home in Leitrim, Michael Harding is faced with the realities of caring for himself for the first time since his illness two years before. Harding endeavours to tame the 'elephant' – an Asian metaphor for the unruly mind. And, as he does, he finds himself finally coming to terms with the death of his mother – a loss that has changed him more than he knows.

Funny, searingly honest and profound, *Hanging with the Elephant* pulls back the curtain and reveals what it is really like to be alive.